AFRICAN AMERICAN WOMEN
Tapping Power and Spiritual Wellness

AFRICAN AMERICAN WOMEN
Tapping Power and Spiritual Wellness

Stephanie Y. Mitchem

THE
PILGRIM
PRESS
Cleveland

There were three African American women who were particularly important in my life. Their processes of dying shape this book about African American women's lives, especially spirituality and health. I dedicate this book to:

My mother,
whose dying process led to the healing of our relationship. She taught me the importance of grace over resignation in the processes of dying.

Aunt Maggie,
mother of my heart, for whom illness and old age became a descent into bitterness. She taught me the importance of cleansing anger in the processes of living.

Daria,
courageous while dying from cancer at a young age. She taught me the importance of risk and the need to be foolish whenever necessary.

The Pilgrim Press, 700 Prospect Avenue
Cleveland, Ohio 44115-1100
thepilgrimpress.com

© 2004 by Stephanie Y. Mitchem

All rights reserved. Published 2004

Printed in the United States of America on acid-free paper

09   08   07   06   05   04   5   4   3   2   1

Library of Congress Cataloging-in-Publication Data
Mitchem, Stephanie Y., 1950-
    African American women tapping power and spiritual wellness / Stephanie Y. Mitchem.
        p. cm.
    Includes bibliographical references and index.
    ISBN 0-8298-1559-7 (pbk. : alk. paper)
    1. African American women – Religious life. 2. Health – Religious aspects – Christianity. 3. African American women – Health and hygiene. 4. Womanist theology.   I. Title.
BR563.N4M59 2004
230'.082'0973 – dc22

2004057305

Contents

PREFACE

I was such an unhealthy person at a very young age. When I say unhealthy, you asked about the mental? Honey, I was laughing, saying as an African American in this country, I been crazy. I mean, didn't have nowhere to go but up. As a young woman, I was very much disrupted, my physical health was in bad shape, I was mentally distraught, and spiritually drained. So I had to make an effort to just work at that. . . . And so through that, I decided I was going to start thinking positive. It doesn't matter what's going on, it doesn't mean that there aren't bad things happening, but I'm going to try to see, okay, what do I get out of this? . . . And I've come to learn attitude is really important for your health, for your physical health.
— AZANA, interviewed in Detroit, 1997

For African American women, tapping is an apt image for experiences of relating to power. Tapping can be a gentle, but persistent way of garnering attention. Tapping can be soothing, but can also become an annoyance. African American women learn early in life by observing the behavior of women in our communities what it means to tap for attention. Tapping can also refer to tapping into some other source of authority or power. Tapped *into* and *on* by African American women, both healing and spirituality are viewed distinctively. In a similar manner, as ideas of healing and spirituality have some distinctive aspects for African American women, so does power. To have power is a person's ability to have some level of control over her or his life. For many African American women, their families, and even neighborhoods, such control is wrested out of their hands. Further, black communities are suspected of crime and moral weakness by the general American public, fueled by media images that are significantly controlled by a small group of nonblacks. As a result of the lack of power, African American women find, name, and use power in ways that are sometimes counter to the mainstream culture.

This book is an exploration of African American women's religious meanings, beginning with the very material realities of health and well-being. Throughout this book, health is understood from the vantage point of wellness, adopting the perspective of the National Black Women's Health Project (NBWHP). The NBWHP defines health as

> not merely the absence of illness, but the active promotion of emotional, mental and physical wellness of this and future generations. Such wellness is impossible without individual and group empowerment. Such personal and collective empowerment is essential to the redefining and reinterpretation of who Black women are, were and can become.[1]

Healing and spirituality are action terms that are part of the processes of learning to tap power and become healthy. My own life attests to the importance of the concepts behind learning to tap power.

Thirty years ago, I was homeless. Twenty years ago, I was an unemployed, single African American mother. Fifteen years ago, I was beginning a master's program, earning the grand sum of $14,000 per year. Each of these moments of my life story carried sets of stereotypes that also indicated my social value in the United States. Today, my life experiences form an important personal basis for this study of African American women's spirituality and healing.

Since the 1950s, social changes have rocketed through the United States with such speed as to leave many of its poorer, less educated citizens behind. Following the Civil Rights Movement of the '60s there was what appeared to be an upturn in socioeconomic gains for African Americans. However, African Americans have never had the amount of social privilege or wealth that ensures adaptability. In the midst of these rapid changes, African Americans have had few role models and fewer mentors to assist in political and social transitions. News reports still list "black firsts," social achievements indicating some movement of black citizens into mainstream American society. Yet these firsts cannot keep up with the rapid pace of social changes. In the social shifts, African Americans — women and men — are confronted with some of the same questions as other Americans. "How do I take care of my aging parents? What child care arrangements do I need to make? Which high school can my child attend?" But there are other questions that white Americans do not need to address. "How should I relate to the African American community if I achieve something? In this work setting, am I acting too 'black'? What do I do to fit into America? What part of myself do I give up?" These daily realities of being African and American are draining and stressful, adding to the burdens of becoming and staying healthy. African American women, who have a significant share of the care of families, must try to answer these questions for themselves and others. African American women are challenged by webs of race and class and gender while attempting to grasp answers.

My professional motivation for writing this book is rooted in years of frustration while I was a student. For example, while attending the seminary in Detroit in the early 1980s, I encountered one white feminist professor who claimed that African American women had not written theology and that the feminist movement began because women wanted to get out of their homes. In both assertions, the woman neatly excluded the participation of African American women from theology (because they wrote nothing) and from feminist dialogues (because they were not worried about liberation from the house). Through these and other encounters that negated my life, I became angry enough to look outside the seminary walls for the religious, social, and political meanings of African American women, worlds of meaning that were completely ignored within academia.

My family and community had meaning worlds. In my time of homelessness and unemployment, I encountered other meaning worlds. It seemed that anything that came from the meaning worlds of black or poor people had little relevance in the rarefied air of the seminary, unless charity (what *we* do for *them*) was the topic. The meanings of African American women were woven into our daily lives. These meanings informed how we as children related to strangers and to each other, learned to define the valuable or the beautiful, and were taught how to pray. Some of the meanings grew from folk wisdom that later helped me survive in some terrible situations. I never accepted that the meanings of African American women's lives were unimportant in theology; instead there seemed to be something missing from the academics' books.

Not only seminaries refused to recognize the meanings of African American women's lives. Churches held few opportunities to address the issues and questions that were part of African American women's meaning worlds. In the churches I attended, preachers did not address gender or class, which, I imagine, were deemed personal or discomfiting issues that did not help congregations feel happy. Sometimes race was discussed, but, again, it seemed distant from my experiences. Churches could have been a place to provide information about African Americans' daily lives and meanings. Instead, "religion" was cleanly amputated from the race-class-gender grit of daily life, except to suggest prayer as a way to get over "those" problems. Both churches and seminaries, I later came to understand, were silent on but still enacting scripts of race, gender, and class. For instance, I once worked with a drug prevention program in which we attempted to get churches to participate. A prominent black church's board, located in a poor, crime-ridden community, politely informed me that there was no need to participate since none of their members had drug problems.

African American Women Tapping Power and Spiritual Wellness is about the meanings of African American women's lives. Healing and spirituality are central to those meanings. In order to achieve a clearer view of these meanings, familial and personal relationships of African American women are the primary lenses through which healing and spirituality are explored. This book focuses on African American women's experiences and meanings in connection with the wider American structures. Such a focus becomes a problem in many ways. For instance, there are portions of the text with which men or women of other cultures and races can identify. Should this book aim for greater inclusivity? Part of the problem of an African American woman writing this kind of analysis is captured by black feminist social critic Michele Wallace. Wallace explored the idea of negation as a primary way that African American women are excluded from research: "What interests me is the problem of a black female cultural perspective, which for the most part is not allowed to become written in a society in which writing is the primary currency of knowledge."[2] So much from the perspectives of African American women is not readily accessible; hence I was informed in seminary that black women had not written theology. African American women, therefore, learn to find ways around the negations. "Variations on negation confront 'the impossible,' the radical being and not-being of women of color."[3] *African American Women Tapping Power and Spiritual Wellness* analyzes how African American women have learned several variations on negations of our spirits and bodies. This book does not answer all questions, but aims to contribute language and vision to womanist work.

Womanist theology and ethics have been under development by African American women since the 1980s. African American women in ethics and theology began to use the term "womanist," adopted from Alice Walker's definition.[4] Walker defined womanists as "black feminists" but further defined other aspects of African American women's lives as constitutive to our self-understandings. For black women, especially those working in ethics and theology, womanist thought became an important way of clarifying who we are, not only for ourselves, but for other African American women in churches. Central to the constructions of womanist theology are experiences of African American women. The processes of constructing theology using African American women's experiences have been rich. But often, writing about African American women requires beginning from unspoken or understated meanings. Thus, *African American Women Tapping Power and Spiritual Wellness* engages African American women's spirituality from the experiential base of healing.

Healing and related health concepts are locations where African American people's spirituality, especially women's, is manifest. Various African American spiritual groundings and practices, informed by many shapes of culture, are found in the nexus of healing and health. Of course, these may vary from region to region, or by faith confessions, classes, or educational levels. However, the constant factor is the frequency with which these different-from-white-cultures' meanings of healing occur, exhibited by the very persistence with which African American women and men have held forms of culture as power to be tapped.

For African American women, tapping power involves the engagement of a form of cultural creativity to take control of their own lives. There are multiple ways that power is created in order to manage situations in life. Because power has been denied them on so many levels in American society, African American women redraw the boundaries of who and what the powerful are, framing discussions of power in ways that renegotiate their own roles in the world. Not merely a salve for the ego, tapping power becomes reality, forming communities, raising families, finding jobs, and improving lives. Power is tapped through resistant and defiant language. Power is tapped through multiple refusals to just quit. Not reduced to ideas of domination, power becomes a spiritual quest.

Spirituality is understood in this book in its most expansive form: spirituality is the total way of being in the world, including the processes of coming to belief systems, naming core values, and acting on those beliefs. Spirituality, in this sense, is not only those components that are bounded by a given denomination or religion. Rather, understood in this way, spirituality can incorporate structures of organized religion as well as go outside those parameters. This definition locates a person in a social milieu in relationship with given communities. Most important, spirituality in this sense gives room to explore the existent framework of the faith beliefs. There are several reasons for defining spirituality in this wide frame.

When definitions of spirituality are limited to those of a given denomination, the other aspects of a human person or community are excluded as tangential. According to some constructions of spirituality, a genuinely Christian person — female, male, young, old, black, white, rich, or poor — should fit into this undifferentiated model. Such a view denies distinctions between persons for the sake of a false Christian "unity" and implies that spirituality itself lacks a cultural referent. True believers, in this view, must conform to the approved mode of spirituality. In fact, much of what dominates as Christian spirituality in the United States draws from a selective Western knowledge base that gives preferential treatment to white views. The wider view of spirituality adopted in this book challenges the Western inbreeding of what is too often defined as mainstream Christian spirituality. Most importantly, at the same time, the wider view gives new ground on which to recognize and define African American women's spirituality.

African American women have been squeezed into definitions of Christianity and spirituality that are wrong-sized. *African American Women Tapping Power and Spiritual Wellness* aims to begin correcting the fit of naming African American women's spirituality. This book participates in the constructions of womanist theology and the analyses of black women's religiosity.

Womanist theologians and ethicists strive to include the personal, the political, the material, and the real, not to expose, but to disclose. The process of disclosure also stresses one problem in this writing: I am part of these communities but stand at a distance to tell the stories; I stand within the community even as I apply the analytical processes I learned in three seminaries. What about the claims of objectivity in scholarship? Contemporary work has shown that there has never been objectivity; each researcher enters with a perspective formed from one's own culture and socialization that influences the resulting theories. Part of the work of this book, especially using African American women's stories, is to reconfigure theories where one set of definitions of reality becomes a clanging dissonance to somebody else's truth.

The conscious connection of these stories with academic theories also supports the validity of the intellectual lives of African American women, whether or not they are in the academy. The purpose of including the words of "everyday" women is to keep this book grounded. The women I spoke with have shaped my writing. The women whom I interviewed were eloquent in speaking their own lives. Certainly, these women cannot speak for all African American women, but certain themes surface and give rise to other ideas.

African American Women Tapping Power and Spiritual Wellness proceeds to look at healing and spirituality from the perspectives of African American women. Chapter 1 explores African American women's health realities in the twenty-first century, quality of life issues that produce or limit well-being. Chapter 1 deals with the data of history and demographics in order to establish the contexts in which African American women frame their own lives. Chapters 2 through 5 examine relationships as core to understanding the lives of African American women. Wellness and religious customs, body and soul, are uncovered or expressed through relationships, a different route to understanding African American women's health issues or practices. Chapter 2 reflects on the images of Mama and Auntie, expressions of mothering that have been centers of healing in African American communities. Chapter 3 explores the historic role of granny midwives and links past healing practices to the present ways that girlfriends can function in African American communities. Chapters 4 and 5 investigate aspects of African American women's sexualities, especially the multiple ways that intimate relationships are in need of healing. Chapter 6 widens the lens to view some aspects of African American communities', especially women's, difficult relationships with health care institutions. This chapter incorporates historical and contemporary perspectives. The concluding chapter gathers components from other chapters to discuss embodied spirituality as tapping power.

African American Women Tapping Power and Spiritual Wellness does not exhaust African American women's meanings with regard to healing and spirituality. But it explores the dance with power that African American women engage, where negative self-interpretations can be denied and faith may be tapped. *African American Women Tapping Power and Spiritual Wellness* is an untold story of the meaning worlds of African American women in the United States.

Acknowledgments

Several people were immensely supportive while I was writing this book. The women who allowed me to interview them must be mentioned first, because they so willingly shared their pain, joy, and insight about African American women's lives. My editor, Kim Sadler, encouraged me to be true to my own voice with her initial, difficult, and necessary questions. Dorita and Delores are friends who asked another important question: "Why don't you tell stories of African American women?" My daughter Barbra cheered me on multiple times, and we have the long distance bills to prove it. Maryann Hazen read through many drafts of the book. Donzetta Jones's wisdom kept me on track. My invaluable Women's Studies colleagues at University of Detroit Mercy, especially Gloria Albrecht and Jane Schaberg, kept me sane with their ongoing support, dinners, and laughter. All of you have my deepest gratitude.

AFRICAN AMERICAN WOMEN

Tapping Power and Spiritual Wellness

ONE

PRELUDE TO TAPPING POWER: JUGGLING ACTS

They're depressed, they're — what do they call it now? — they're stressed. Stressed used to be a cup of ginger tea when I was coming along. Make you some ginger tea, girl, and lay down. Be all right. Now it's big-time stress. It causes their understanding to be limited because there's a blockage there. . . . That's one reason I am so intolerant of women and cramps. Why should a woman be off two days a month for cramps? I don't understand that. Put you some ginger tea in your coffee maker. You'll be okay.

—QUINCY, interviewed in Detroit, 1997

As a prelude, this chapter is foundational to those succeeding because it sketches the social underpinnings and material realities that contribute to different views of spirituality and healing that African American women hold. In order to understand the meanings and acts of tapping power, it is necessary to lay the groundwork. What historical situations led to the development of present conditions? What, exactly, are African American women encountering that necessitates tapping power?

Today, America generally accepts historically invented, well-promoted myths about what it means to be citizens in the U.S. The myths center on equality and opportunity for everyone who "works hard." Opportunities, the myths claim, are available for all citizens today. Therefore, it is believed that any individual or community unwilling to work hard should not be encouraged in their

3

laziness by taking bread they do not deserve from the mouths of those deserving people who do work. Hence the drive to end social "entitlements" such as welfare became popular arguments for politicians: the propaganda of supposed unfair taxation of the industrious to support the indolent became a successful ploy that used the poor to get politicians elected.

From this politicized perspective, success must be earned. The United States' social culture proclaims itself to be a meritocracy: all good deeds by worthy persons, regardless of race, class, or gender, will be rewarded. The few visible faces of color in politics, entertainment, and business are displayed as a way to validate this story: these "good" people worked hard and received their deserved rewards. Further, the few dark faces validate another related American tale: set-aside preferences are unnecessary for African American people. The success of immigrant groups, like some Irish or Italians, supports the erroneous, but popular belief that because *they* worked hard and were successful, any other group should be able to achieve. Some contend, surely, any continued lack of success that African American women and men experience is a result of their limited abilities, lack of intelligence, and refusal to work hard.

This propaganda is popular and pervasive. The myths are easily accepted by the general public, including many African Americans. Oprah's rich, Venus and Serena are tennis stars, and Condoleezza's running around the White House. Who can believe that African American women have problems, except of their own making, in this day and age of opportunity? Factually, there is only a small percentage of Americans for whom the fairy stories about merit-for-hard-work actually fit. Many other people do not analyze at whose expense their families achieved wealth in this country. For whatever reasons, acceptance of the myths of opportunity in America is widespread and appealing. After all, myths invite us to believe and be comfortable. Yet, for most African Americans, facile acceptance of these myths is quickly destroyed by the realities of daily life.

The state of African American women's well-being in the United States is fraught with contradictions and conflicts. Foremost among the issues for consideration is the debilitating combination of race, class, and gender in African American women's lives. Not singly race *or* class *or* gender, but all together shape African American women's realities. Gender, race, and class combine to multiply their effects on life. These three are complicated by additional layers of social conditions that may further affect a woman's status, such as physical ability, sexual preference, and mental capacity. As African American women analyze oppression, these multiple social layers must be taken into account. The experiences of oppression are not abstractions; they actually impact African American women's material realities, their mental, economic, physical, and spiritual health.

The three sections in this chapter investigate the impact of these experiences on African American women's lives. Section one traces the historical and contemporary realities of African American women's bodies as colonized. How have the years of enslavement and Jim Crowism impacted current challenges? The second section of the chapter addresses African American women's health in general terms. What are the conditions that impact health at the beginning of the twenty-first century? The third section considers the concepts of embodied spirituality as central to womanist theological work.

African American Women's Bodies, Colonized

The contemporary stories of African American women's experiences of oppression are connected with the past. Commencing a study of healing and spirituality begins with the historical contexts. From the arrival of Africans in America, African bodies were viewed as part of the wealth to be conquered. Such thinking was visually constructed in the sixteenth and seventeenth centuries when mapmakers used women's bodies as symbols for continents. Unlike the other symbolized women, clothed as goddesses, "Africa" was depicted as a naked black woman.

In the American colonies, dominated African bodies were an integral part of building the country that would become the United

States. Yet, making slaves was not simply a matter of picking up some Africans and shipping them to a new land. Historian Walter Johnson dissects the experiences of enslavement in antebellum Louisiana. He describes the process of turning people into things or products. "From an early age slaves' bodies were shaped to their slavery. . . . Through care and discipline, slaves' bodies were physically incorporated with their owners' standards of measure."[1] Enslavement was not invented by the Americas, but the chattel principle was a novel feature that led to innovative levels of dehumanization. People were turned into marketable products, marketed through the sales pitches of the traders.[2] With black bodies as commodities, it was expected that the "products" were transparently of monetary value: physical vitality indicated a "good" slave product; scarred bodies indicated whipping and "bad" slave merchandise. African women's breasts and stomachs were manipulated, as their worth was tied to "breeding" capability. "As slaveholders looked over the people they bought to cook their meals, wash their clothes, and wait on their tables, they elaborated fantasies about their slaves' interior lives and intellectual capacity."[3] As Johnson states, the process of making people into products was not one into which enslaved African people went quietly. Rather there was resistance by African American people against being turned into disposable goods.

> Whether they were sold for speculation, debt or punishment, many slaves refused to go quietly. They disrupted their sales in both philosophy and practice. In philosophy by refusing to accept their owners' account of what was happening, by treating events that slaveholders described in the language of economic necessity or disciplinary exigency as human tragedy or personal betrayal. In practice by running away or otherwise resisting their sale, forcing their owners to create public knowledge of the violent underpinnings of their power. . . . These were the "many thousands gone" memorialized in the stories and songs of which antebellum slaves built a systematic critique of the institution under which they lived.[4]

The processes of making slaves included issues of health. Historian Sharla Fett noted the integration of medicine and slavery when "professional southern doctors defended the merits of southern medical science by proclaiming a new domain of race- and region-specific medicine that reinforced emergent proslavery ideology."[5] The tropical climate of the South was considered unhealthy; yellow fever, malaria, typhoid fever, "tuberculosis, and a host of other diseases kept the death rate high. . . . It is estimated that work days lost to illness were four times greater in the South than in the North."[6] Southern physicians claimed that the region itself — hotter and wetter — was a major factor when making the comparison. If African Americans were stricken with different diseases and higher death rates than white people, it was argued by some white physicians that race naturally made the distinction in biological structures and responses. An example was Samuel Cartwright, an eighteenth-century white physician, who was considered a leader in "what has been called 'States Rights medicine.'" He went so far as to label two slave-specific diseases: drapetomania, the primary symptom of which was the attempted or real escape of a slave "from service"; and dysesthesia aethiopis, for which "frivolity" and "rascality" were symptoms.[7]

Within the context of the African communities' levels of risk, African women's bodies in the world of enslavement were defined in terms of their uses. Or, as womanist theologian M. Shawn Copeland emphasizes, African women under enslavement were especially demeaned. "The black woman was reduced to body parts — parts which allowed white men pleasure, however unsettling; parts which afforded white men economic gain; parts which literally nursed the heirs to white racist supremacy."[8] Besides the use of African American women's bodies for the immediate comfort of white people, they were also subject to experimentation by white physicians. African American feminist anthropologist Cheryl Mwaria noted that slaves were accessible subjects for study: the only consent needed was from the owner who stood to gain a profit from the medical doctor; mistakes were disregarded. Mwaria indicates two such medical developments, one of caesarean section for the delivery of a child and another, the surgical procedure for alleviating vesico-vaginal fistulas (urine or feces leaks through the vaginal opening).[9] Mwaria stated that these practices were quite widespread:

> Although there is much documented evidence of the use of slaves, especially women, as subjects of medical experimentation, it by no means represents an exhaustive list of these practices. Many physicians and lay practitioners of medicine experimented on slaves without recording their results. Some documented experiments presaged those of the Nazi doctors, such as those designed to see if Blacks could withstand more pain or depletion than Whites.[10]

The story of the colonization of African American women's and men's bodies did not end with the Emancipation Proclamation of the 1860s. Legal enslavement ended but the processes of colonizing black bodies continued. The white population of North and South expected the extinction of black people at slavery's end: who would "take care" of those infantile, ignorant black people? Enslavement's chattel principle only shifted how it was stated, but the principle did not depart the popular mind-set. Historian Richard Meckel demonstrates these connections in his discussion of infant mortality rates following Emancipation.

> Focusing on the causes and rates of death among African American infants, this discourse originated from racialist debates on the social, moral and health impact of emancipation and the consequent migration of blacks to southern cities. Much of it was *dominated by the views of southern physicians and public health officials who, by virtue of the concentration of the African American population in the south, assumed a type of proprietary expertise in all matters relating to black morbidity and mortality.* [emphasis added][11]

For African Americans, hospitals, during and after slavery, were viewed as places of terror, not healing. Medical experiments on African Americans continued beyond slavery's ending, especially as professional medicine was being developed. "Night doctors" were particularly feared by African Americans.

> Night doctors were medical students, or those in the employ of medical students, who went out during the night to abduct people and take them back to hospitals, where they were used in experiments before being killed. Fear of the night doctors was so pervasive in black communities in the South that throughout much of the nineteenth and early twentieth centuries people would avoid being out at night alone in the vicinity of a hospital.[12]

In a climate that disregarded black lives, controlling African American bodies became a feature of the American landscape. That disregard was shown through the lynching and raping of African American men and women that blatantly continued through the mid-twentieth century. Contemporary historian Grace Elizabeth Hale points out that lynching African Americans served to define whiteness.

> "Lynch carnivals," as a popular book on the subject written in the 1930s described them, were rituals increasingly bound up with the way southern whites shaped the practices of modern consumption to their own ends, communal spectacles of torture that helped ease white fears of a raceless consumer society even as they helped structure segregation. . . . Publicly resolving the race, gender, and class ambiguities at the very center of the culture of segregation, spectacle lynchings brutally conjured a collective, all-powerful whiteness even as they made the color line seem modern, civilized, and sane. Spectacle lynchings were about making racial difference in the new South, about ensuring the separation of all southern life into whiteness and blackness.[13]

Fear for physical well-being, absence of security, and the threat of exploitation came to represent the general state of black life in the United States. Such a climate has had a profound impact on African

Americans. "Misogyny and violence have deformed our imaginations. They leave us discouraged, dispirited, and numb; wounded culturally and socially, psychically and physically, morally and religiously."[14] In an account of African American mental health, two researchers explained the long-term impact of these experiences through the concept of "posttraumatic slavery syndrome." Specifically, a culture of oppression, the byproduct of this nation's development, has taken a tremendous toll on the minds and bodies of black people.[15]

For African American women, the impact of the American longitudinal study in human terror has yet to be fully understood. Some questions by African American feminist historian Adrienne Davis make this connection to African American women's lives today:

> Have we, today, fully reclaimed our own intimate lives from that horror [of the past]? What are the ongoing effects of slavery's systemic expropriation of black women's reproduction and sexuality for market and political purposes? How does the sexual economy of slavery continue to affect the policing of black women's sexuality?[16]

Through the eighteenth and nineteenth centuries, the human body became a tool for studying people. The "scientific" definitions of races and bodies established the body types and the groups of people that were to be deemed normal and those that were condemned as pathological. From these earlier centuries, body-reading became embedded in American society in countless ways. People are critically judged on looks — race being a significant factor. In judgments-by-race, black people do not fit the model. Such judgments are one signal of the continued presence of a colonized mind-set. There is a rhyme from African American communities that demonstrated the preference of white skin over black: "If you're white, you're all right. If you're brown, stick around. If you're black, get back." One author, Sarah Chinn, stated: "The valuation of whiteness and of sexual chastity in a racially asymmetrical and hierarchically gendered world was translated into the moral and aesthetic imperative of a lily-white complexion through which the 'spotless' soul was easily legible."[17]

Specific analysis of the idea of colonizing African American women's bodies is discussed in chapter 4. However, the groundings of tapping power need further description. The framework of African American women's health is another component that distinguishes their understandings of healing and spirituality.

African American Women's Health Realities

Racism... it's just so much a part of our life it makes me sick. From racism — and I put this under racism cause it's all part of racism — it's expected that you give 110 percent. It doesn't matter if you're just as smart as the other two white women, you've got to be two times smarter than them to get equal respect.... It's just crazy. You have to live in two worlds; if you work around whites then you're home with your family.... You have to find a way to work and proceed in the world, to have self-confidence and know who you are.... I don't want to be negative [laughs] but... that's where internal healing comes in, because you have to find a way to work and proceed in this world, know who you are, and know that the change is so gradual, so gradual, it probably won't happen in your lifetime.   — MELODY, interviewed in Detroit, 1997

One common method of considering African Americans' health issues has been to look at the numbers. According to the U.S. Census of 2000, there were in that year 36,419,434 black Americans. The number includes both those who filled in the form with only black or a combination of black with another ethnic group.[18] Black Americans now compose 12.9 percent of the U.S. population, with the highest concentration in twenty-two states. Detroit, a source of interviews for *African American Women Tapping Power and Spiritual Wellness,* is a city with the third-largest urban concentration of African Americans, superseded only by New York and Chicago.

The numbers from the 2000 Census can be interpreted in different ways. For instance, the Census Bureau itself sent out a press release for African American History Month in February 2002 presenting a decidedly upbeat spin on the information.[19]

> $30,439 [indicates] the 2000 median income of African American households, which is a new all-time high ... 22.1 percent [indicates] poverty rate for African Americans in 2000 ... down from 23.6 percent in 1999. About a half-million fewer African Americans were poor in 2000 ... 79 percent [indicates] the proportion of African Americans age 25 and over who were high school graduates in 2000 — a record high ... 17 percent [indicates] the percentage of African Americans age 25 and over with at least a bachelor's degree in 2000 — a record high.[20]

The optimistic interpretation of the numbers signals a time-cures-all approach to long-standing racial disparities, implying that African Americans' problems will surely go away as they advance in U.S. society. This interpretation is reminiscent of old arguments against any social change that would benefit African Americans because some kind of social evolutionary process would end enslavement or bring about civil rights. Today, another implication from the positive interpretation is that African American success stories prove that working hard has results, and those who don't work hard will fail. These positive interpretations serve to give comfort to the already comfortable in American society, avoiding any deeper analysis of U.S. social and political structures and thereby avoiding any social changes. Easy readings of the numbers of the 2000 Census do not present true pictures of who African Americans are or how we live. Questions need answers that would disclose realities beyond the statistics. What does it mean to make a living as an African American in the United States? In African American communities, what is the level of access to services and goods? Do institutions, from banks to schools, present blockages to community growth? Are African American communities still red-lined? Is

TABLE 1:
LIFE EXPECTANCY AT BIRTH, SELECTED YEARS

Birth year	Black male	Black female	White female	White male
1900	32.5	33.5	48.7	46.6
1950	59.1	62.9	72.2	66.5
1960	61.1	66.3	72.2	66.5
1970	60.0	68.3	75.6	68.0
1980	63.8	72.5	78.1	70.7
1990	64.5	73.6	79.4	72.7
1995	65.2	73.9	79.6	73.4
1999	67.8	74.7	79.9	74.6

Source: National Center for Health Statistics, United States, 2002 with Chartbook on Trends in the Health of Americans (Hyattsville, Md., 2002), 116. (Order adjusted from original table to present black and white females' data adjoined)

there still institutional racism? How do these impact the quality of life?

There are other numbers that can be considered when drawing a picture of African American health conditions. By widening the viewing lens and particularly taking into account the numbers following 2001's recession, a different picture of African American life is drawn that is not so idyllic. Among the statistics that can be explored are life expectancy, illness, treatment, and economic conditions.

Life expectancy is an important measure by which much can be determined. African American women's life expectancy has dramatically increased over the last century (see Table 1). In 1900 the average life expectancy for black women was 33.5 years; by 1999, it had risen to 74.7 years. Yet a gap remains between black and white women's life expectancy rates. In 1900 the life expectancy of white women exceeded black women by 15 years; by 1999 the gap had narrowed to 5 years. On the surface, this is good news; on another, the persistence of the gap raises the question of "why does it remain?" Despite the interpretations of increased life expectancy, the quality of African American women's lives cannot be determined solely by the quantity of years.

When considering illness and treatment related to life expectancy, other gaps in services that health care institutions provide become clearer. Nationally, as one example, between 1989 and 1997, there was a thirteen-point gap between African American and white women in the survival rates for all types of cancer. That difference in African American and white women's cancer survival actually widened by two points from 1980.[21] In another example the possibility of maternal mortality from complications of pregnancy, childbirth, and their aftermath has been four times higher for African American than white women between 1990 and 1999.[22] Or consider that from 1985 through June 2001, of all women with acquired immunodeficiency syndrome (AIDS), 22.5 percent are white and 60.5 percent are African American women.[23] Why are these differences so drastic? Very few studies explore questions like these, preferring the comfortable interpretation of statistics over the deeper analysis.

One reason for the preference is suggested through the work of Jacqueline Battalora, a white ethicist and attorney, who provides a sharp analysis to the ideals of whiteness in American society. Considering the operations of white privilege, she used the statement, "I can be pretty sure that studies of diseases and disorders and of their medical treatments include a significant percentage of people from my racial group."[24] African Americans do not have that comfort. A razor-sharp difference is seen when studies are done from African American perspectives, especially when determining the impact of racism on health. Studies like these are beginning, but some researchers at the University of Michigan gathered information already available.

> Initially, institutional racial discrimination may affect the actual living conditions of black Americans and lead to environmental deprivation. This influences the presence and quality of health care, and introduces various stressors for black Americans. As a result, some black Americans may adopt behavioral coping responses such as poor nutritional habits or substance abuse that are detrimental to health. Moreover, the perception of racial discrimination also invokes behavioral coping responses such as cigarette smoking or

alcohol use, which increase risks of chemical dependency and various forms of cancer. The individual perceptions of racial discrimination may also alter negatively the quality of life of black Americans ... [as in] low levels of life satisfaction and personal happiness because of environmental demands that exceed individual coping capacity.[25]

Income is another factor that can be considered in analyzing African Americans' health. The importance of understanding relationships between health and income surfaced in another study from the Program for Research on Black Americans. In a study about connections between health and self esteem, the researcher made some connections with financial well-being.

Building upon the body of research that self-esteem is one of the most important aspects of emotional well-being, the present study shows that blacks' self-assessed health significantly affects how they evaluate their definition of self.... Although not the primary focus of this study, *financial stress was significantly associated with lower levels of self-esteem. ... Therefore it is no surprise that in a society where financial success often determines individuals' sense of worth, financial stress is negatively associated with the self-esteem of African Americans.*[26]

Such financial stressors are made clear when statistics about income are contemplated. African American households generally lost income between 2000 and 2001, with married couples and female householders experiencing a slight increase (see Table 2 on the following page). The median incomes shown for African American households stand in stark contrast with white households, where the median income is higher (see Table 3).

A nagging $15,000 gap between African American and white median incomes in all households remained from 2000 to 2001. Overall, in all categories, white Americans earned more than African Americans. One area of note is the difference between

TABLE 2:
BLACK AMERICANS' MEDIAN INCOME,
TWO-YEAR COMPARISON

	2001 median income		2000 median income	
	Number (1,000)	Value (dollars)	Number (1,000)	Value (dollars)
All households	13,315	29,470	13,174	29,667
Family households	8,844	35,080	8,731	35,577
Married couples	4,233	51,557	4,214	50,692
Male householders (no wife present)	733	34,540	732	38,276
Female householders (no husband present)	3,838	22,059	3,785	21,521

Source: U.S. Census Bureau, "Income 2001: Table 1, Median Income of Households by Selected Characteristics, Race, and Hispanic Origin of Householder," www.census.gov/hhes/income.

TABLE 3:
WHITE AMERICANS' MEDIAN INCOME,
TWO-YEAR COMPARISON

	2001 median income		2000 median income	
	Number (1,000)	Value (dollars)	Number (1,000)	Value (dollars)
All households	90,682	44,517	90,030	43,916
Family households	61,638	55,051	61,320	54,043
Married couple families	49,605	61,137	49,468	59,957
Male householders (no wife present)	3,394	41,680	3,280	43,403
Female householders (no husband present)	8,639	31,132	8,753	31,295

Source: U.S. Census Bureau, "Income 2001: Table 1, Median Income of Households by Selected Characteristics, Race, and Hispanic Origin of Householder," www.census.gov/hhes/income.

African American and white female householders with no husband present. African American female householders have a median income that is $9,000 less than white women in the same category. Additionally, the longer life expectancy of white women and the

TABLE 4:
SAMPLE OF BLACK AMERICANS' EMPLOYMENT SHIFTS, NOVEMBER 2001 AND NOVEMBER 2002

SELECTED OCCUPATIONS (by percentages)	WOMEN			MEN		
	Nov. 2001	Nov. 2002	+/-	Nov. 2001	Nov. 2002	+/-
Executive, administrative	11.1	10.7	−0.4	9.2	9.1	−0.1
Professional specialty	15.1	15.0	−0.1	10.2	9.2	−1.0
Technicians and related support	3.6	3.5	−0.1	2.1	2.6	+0.5
Sales occupations	12.0	10.8	−1.2	8.1	7.4	−0.7
Administrative support, including clerical	23.9	23.5	−0.4	8.3	9.1	+0.8
Service, private household	0.8	1.2	+0.4	N/A	N/A	
Service, protective	1.9	1.9	0.0	5.8	5.7	−0.1
Service, except household or private	21.8	23.4	+1.6	12.4	13.1	+0.7
Precision production, craft, repair	1.6	1.7	+0.1	13.6	13.6	0.0
Machine operators, assemblers	4.5	4.5	0.0	8.0	7.9	−0.1
Transportation, material moving	1.7	1.6	−0.1	10.6	10.8	+0.2
Handlers, helpers, laborers	1.8	2.0	+0.2	2.0	2.2	+0.2
Farming, forestry, fishing	0.2	0.1	−0.1	2.0	2.2	+0.2

Source: U.S. Bureau of Labor Statistics, "Household Data not seasonally adjusted, Table A 20." See ftp://ftp.bls.gov/pub/suppl/empsit.cpseea20.txt.

greater earnings of their families over time indicate greater lifetime resources and earnings that could be passed to succeeding generations, thereby maintaining and strengthening their social position. In other words, African American families work harder, live shorter lives, and receive fewer benefits. These are socially structured conditions that promote ill health.

Numbers from the Bureau of Labor Statistics provide even stronger images of the economic gaps between African Americans and white Americans. The numbers show that the American economic recession has had a decided impact on African Americans' earnings (see Table 4). Out of thirteen occupational categories, African American women lost ground in all but four areas. For the higher earning categories, particularly administration, African American women held fewer positions in November 2002 than the previous year. More light is shed on these disparities when issues of health are discussed.

The U.S. Center for Disease Control and the National Center for Health Statistics have developed "Healthy People 2010," which lists leading indicators of health for all Americans and sets statistical targets for achievement by the year 2010.[27] When considering the categories used by the developers of the indicators, obstructions block African Americans' paths to reaching the healthy goals. The categories encompass, for the most part, standard health practices. The reduction of tobacco use, with an aim by 2010, of lowering to 12 percent the percentage of adults who smoke is one of the categories. Healthy People 2010 aspires to increase the percentage of teens who do not use alcohol or drugs and to decrease the number of adults who binge drink or use illicit drugs. Responsible sexual behavior is called for, with a focus on condom use as a primary measure at all age levels. As a measure of promoting mental health, Healthy People 2010 views an increase in the percentage of those treated for recognized depression as a leading indicator. Environmental quality, indicated by lowered ozone levels and exposure to passive tobacco smoke, is another of the measures. Regular physical activity, for those over fourteen years of age, entails at least twenty minutes of vigorous exercise three times weekly; Healthy People 2010 aims for at least 50 percent of adults to participate by 2010. A variety of issues impact many African Americans' abilities to participate in reaching these goals. Some examples for each category will clarify.

The reduction of tobacco and substance abuse is thwarted by heavy marketing campaigns in many largely African American communities that promote alcohol and tobacco use with the beautiful and happy faces of black models. It is more than marketing: certain types of alcohol are more readily available in African American communities, such as the "forty-ounce" size beer and cheaper brands of liquor that often have higher alcohol content. Some African American communities have attempted to counter this trend with campaigns such as "Denounce the 40 ounce," but these efforts are not nearly as well funded or slickly presented as the liquor companies' promotions.

The promotion of responsible sexual behavior, especially through condom use, presents a quandary in African American communities, where issues of sexuality are compounded by what womanist theologian Kelly Brown Douglas terms a legacy of white sexual assault.[28] The legacy confounds educational efforts, even the ability to discuss sex. Douglas continues: "It would be dishonest to suggest that White culture has not impacted Black sexuality. . . . In the contemporary Black community the jolt of White culture is clear. . . . The White cultural attack . . . has rendered the Black community virtually impotent in its ability to conduct frank, open, and demanding discourse concerning matters of sexuality."[29] For African American women and men, sexuality is a thorny issue related to health, as discussed at length in chapters 4 and 5. The promotion of condom use, called for by Healthy People 2010, cannot address the multiple concerns for healthy sexuality in African American communities.

Emerging from the indicator of promoting mental health through treatment of depression is the general issue of racism among mental health workers and the continual misdiagnosis of African Americans. As clinicians Alvin Poussaint and Amy Alexander noted: "White mental health practitioners — conditioned by years of cultural stereotypes depicting blacks as leading emotionally uncomplicated lives — have trouble acknowledging depression in black Americans. Consequently, severe clinical depression is often underdiagnosed among black Americans."[30] The issues of mental health among African Americans cannot be addressed simply with better diagnoses. Instead, the impact of race and racism needs exploration. "Although it has been argued that race is not important in the psychiatric epidemiological arena, others have shown that the combination of disadvantaged status (whether economic or social disadvantage) and exposure to discrimination increases blacks' susceptibility to psychological distress and mental disorders."[31] Further discussion of African American mental health appears in chapter 6.

Environmental quality is now an additional threat to African Americans in poorer or urban settings. "Members of minority and

poorer communities are more likely to live in polluted environ-
ments and to work in hazardous occupations. There may also be
a disproportionate placement of pollution-intensive industries and
hazardous waste sites in low-income and minority communities."[32]
For instance, Detroit, like other industrial areas, has leftover industrial waste that has been buried in sites from which tire or auto
factories have long moved. The grassroots organization Detroiters
Working for Environmental Justice has been very vocal in attempting to alter these realities and working to educate other local groups
for corrective action, even as they continue to expose the underpinnings of environmental racism. The indicators chosen by Healthy
People 2010 were developed for the general population of the United
States. However, inability to act upon these indicators in African
American communities points to complex webs of social relations.

This brief look at the indicators as they relate to the realities in
black people's lives is blanketed by overall issues of employment
and the possibilities of earning a decent living wage. Employment
will not alone correct the situations described above, and health
will not be a simple and quick result of any job. However, economic
distress adds to health problems. As an example, Detroit with an
83 percent African American population remains economically depressed. One study indicated a 193 percent increase in poverty
between 1980 and 1990, with 40 percent of the city in poverty.[33]
One indicator of social and economic stress is the percentage of
female-headed households in contrast to affluent communities that
have low numbers of female-headed households. The same study
indicates that over 55 percent of households in Detroit, based on
the 1990 Census, are headed by women.[34] The prognosis for social
mobility and accumulation of wealth is not good for black women
residents. Such a prognosis only serves to reiterate one of the health
indicators: access to health care and other benefits of affluence will
be difficult for these women and their children.

The economic decline of Detroit is masked by reports from the
U.S. Department of Statistics that offer a glowing picture of employment in Michigan. According to the statistics, Michigan has

an unemployment rate below the national average: Michigan's rate is 5.7 percent; the nation's is 6 percent.[35] However, the figures do not represent the number of jobless people, only those who have become unemployed within a certain time frame, which allows them to receive unemployment compensation. As a newspaper story pointed out, there is a different reading of unemployment figures. The skewed statistics are nonrepresentative of the misery.

> While the effects of the 2001 recession appear to be easing, economist [sic] say the thousands of Michiganians who have given up looking for work are still in a lot of pain.... The economy isn't rebounding fast enough for some Michiganians.... Around 35,000 in the state will be kicked off a federal extension of unemployment benefits Dec. 28....[36]

This describes some of the parameters of the world in which African American women try today to create health for themselves and their families. In this world, it may be difficult to consider health as anything more than a luxury item. There are significant issues of trust of the professional medical establishment. Black people's circumstances cannot be defined simply by numbers but, too often, policy makers interpret and disseminate their findings with positive interpretations that may best fit their programmatic or budgetary needs. African American people do not define themselves by statistics or numbers. As the African American comedian Sinbad stated, "I didn't know I was poor until I went to college." The particular ways that African American women shape their own definitions of their existence or social location are explored later in the chapter. This shaping of perspective of African American people points to another issue for consideration in this book: how are African American women's bodies understood in American society?

The concepts in the preceding two sections provide context and foundation for this book. However, distinguishing the sources and significance of black women's spirituality is necessary before continuing.

Spirituality and Womanist Work

*It's almost as if black women can worry themselves into bad
health. And that has a lot to do with attitude and how you
think about things. We aren't necessarily problem solvers unless it's somebody else. In other words, we can figure out ways
to get things done for our children, our partners, our families.
We can figure out things for somebody else, but when it's time
to figure out things for ourselves, it's kind of like we get fumbly.
Because we don't necessarily take time to correct it or resolve
it or whatever's necessary. So many times, women are talking
to me about what's going on physically and I consider myself
more of a mirror, . . . and the next question I ask is, "But what
are you going to do about it?"*

— AZANA, interviewed in Detroit, 1997

The information garnered from the numbers provided by the
Census Bureau or Health Department is contingent upon the
interpreter. Azana's statement could be understood varyingly according to the reader's perception. Is she a hard worker? Has she
learned the importance of health care? Deeper analysis would lead
to asking "why" questions. *Why* would African American women
worry themselves into bad health? *Why* would we have difficulty
taking care of ourselves? These are the questions that womanist
theology asks.

Theologies come from faith perspectives. Personal faith comes
from one person's beliefs that are firmly in mind, actions that live
those beliefs, and trust in the ultimate realities behind those beliefs.
Communal faith is shared on different levels, as church groups
or community members. Personal faith is in interaction with the
communal, mutually shaping and influencing each other. Womanist theology is consciously constructed from African American
women's experiences and beliefs. African American women have
found ways to make their church homes into homes for themselves.
But too many churches' theologies, doctrines, rituals, and policies do not resonate with African American women: churches are

skillful at ignoring what they choose to ignore. Womanist theology addresses these issues, bringing our experiences into the forefront instead of the background. Foregrounding might also mean that those churches' theologies, doctrines, rituals, and policies end up getting challenged by new insights. What happens when African American women's experiences are brought to the fore? Race, gender, class, ability, sexual preference, and all of the other experiences of African American women's lives become highlighted in ways that they had never been before. Certainly, most of our experiences with race, gender, class, and ability tend to be negative; too many of our other life experiences are caught up in trying to resist or restructure those oppressive ones.

While dealing with the interlocking oppressions of race, class, and gender, in the middle of the number-driven definitions through which they are viewed, African American women have choices. The choices are not bound by acceptance of limiting roles. African American women may draw from culturally based sources that provide new wells for creativity. In other words, African American women retain human abilities to create options for themselves and their communities. This ability is known as agency. Byllye Avery, the founder of the National Black Women's Health Project, defines agency in nearly spiritual terms. "Each of us has agency. Agency is the power within us to change ourselves and the world around us. Connecting with our sense of agency takes us on a lifelong journey of empowerment — for ourselves and others. Agency is one of our most precious gifts . . . and one of our most awesome responsibilities."[37] Among the sources for personal agency from which African American women draw is spirituality. African American women's spirituality is sometimes referred to as "embodied." Embodied spirituality makes sense on several levels and is discussed in further detail in chapter 7.

The concept of embodied spirituality ties into the historical and continued separation of African American people in the United States. Some sections of the country are today more racially integrated than others. The notion of workplace or college "diversity" is misleading; separations still exist. Some people erroneously believe that integration was the aim of the Civil Rights Movement and, therefore, mark that period of time of the mid-twentieth century as the end of race as a formative issue. But this understanding of the importance of race is superficial and simplistic. From nearly the beginning of African presence in the American colonies, African American people were defined by their inequity to white people. After the emancipation of the enslaved, segregation was made into law and continued to perpetrate a series of social injustices that regulated racial space. Belief in segregation was aided by white theological developments that necessitated the separation of the races as "God's law." African Americans lived under *de jure* or *de facto* segregation until the Supreme Court decision of *Brown v. Board of Education* in 1954. Even after the 1954 court decision, years of struggle for voting and other civil rights followed. It was easy to retain differences in separate but unequal societies. Even though cultural forms that originated among African American people — from music to dress — have been imported into white communities, it remains true that, too often, African Americans continue to be placed in marginal social spaces.

The idea of embodied spirituality indicates a different perspective from the Western notion of sharply defined and separate areas of body and soul. A different anthropology of religion is operating, informed by other cultural values. For instance, Vincent Wimbush's recent studies provide one example of African Americans' use of and relation to the Bible.[38] African American women are informed by cultural and social meanings, including religion, and are shaped by their African American communities. African American women's sense of embodied spirituality is holistic and part of the lives of their communities.

What does it mean to claim that African American women have a holistic sense of spirituality? What are the social dynamics shaping such understandings? Joyce West Stevens has studied the ways that African American girls develop strategies of resistance. She notes that these strategies are necessary because of "racial victimization and gender devaluation." Stevens states:

Black girls' sassy conduct is a central feature of identity exploration. The common inference of sassiness is defiant conduct. Notwithstanding considering a strengths perspective of sassy conduct, a counterpoint inference is candidness, courage, determination, and assertiveness — clearly strengths needed to challenge racial/gender stereotypes and biases and to master bicultural competence. Hypothetically, sassiness can be a promising phase in the development of black girls.[39]

M. Shawn Copeland, womanist theologian, constructed a theology of suffering and explored the importance of sass as "audacious, bold, and willful words that guard identity."[40] There are clearly links that must inform a study of spirituality.

Another developmental focus for African American girls is the importance of mutuality and relationships. As a result of work with African American girls and their mothers in group therapy settings, two researchers observed:

> Although African American girls are encouraged to be strong and self-sufficient, they are also expected to remain connected (closely tied) to their immediate and extended families. . . . Thus, the self-in-relation model with its emphasis on the mother-daughter bond, the importance of connection and the centrality of relationships is especially attractive to African Americans.[41]

From a womanist theological perspective, African American women's spirituality encompasses all of life: work and health are integrated into knowing something about who God is and who we are called to become. Faith is certainly part of this, but commitment, or lack of one, to a single denomination will not end the sense of active, engaged spirituality. Sassiness, strength, resistance, cultural values, mutuality, community, and religiosity all inform spirituality. Here is the sense of spirituality as a way of being in the world, as stated in the introduction. God truly becomes Word in this spirituality: a verb, participating, demanding, and assisting throughout life.

Integral to these components is the female-centered tradition of African American biblical appropriation that has been named by womanist theologian Delores Williams the "survival/quality-of-life tradition." "Even today, most of Hagar's situation is congruent with many African American women. . . . Many black women have testified that 'God helped them make a way out of no way.' "[42] This tradition interacts with and informs the sassiness and cultural values. In other words, if God is present, Jesus is a partner, and the Holy Spirit a moving force, the Bible is one more level of the interactive relationship with the Divine. The partner God communicates through biblical passages. A black woman opening a Bible during times of trouble may seek answers or comfort, feeling either response will be found in the words that God is sending.

Womanist theologian A. Elaine Brown Crawford explored these themes differently with abused African American women's understandings of hope. From this, Crawford constructed statements of a womanist theology of hope: "Hope is the theological construct that moves these [abused] women beyond endurance to survival, and ultimately toward the transformation of oppressive circumstances. Hope is the bridge from oppression to liberation that facilitates full humanity and fosters an undaunted passion for life."[43]

While African American women's spirituality is embodied, at the same time understandings of health are intertwined with spirituality. Historian Sharla Fett, analyzing slave doctoring practices, refers to the importance of collective relationships for healing, relations that went beyond the merely human. "Enslaved healers, working in relationship to this spiritually empowered world, often described their skills as 'gifts' and attributed their knowledge to divine intervention."[44] These historically based concepts still hold sway in many African American communities: circumstances of African American segregation ensured the retention of past practices and knowledge bases.

These ideas are reflected in the words of Byllye Avery.

Spirit gets to the heart of things. Spirit is our inner core, our soul and our psyche. Spirit is the strength that enables us to get things done. It is an internal presence that provides us with faith and courage. . . . Women have a well of spirit to draw on in our families and community. The struggle of Black folk worldwide against racism and oppression speaks to the depths of our spiritual wells. We must draw from them when we feel vulnerable and challenged.[45]

Body and soul are connected, and health is not merely the physical, but incorporates the entire person: family, relationships, economics, mental, spiritual, the past, and the present. The holistic approach to health parallels African American women's understandings of spirituality.

"Tapping power" is an apt phrase to describe African American women's efforts to access health, and refers to a faith relationship with the divine. God's power heals: emotionally, physically, and economically. But power is not only from God. African American women use faith as a route to tapping the power within themselves. These power forms are enhanced through relationships.

Womanist work includes these layers of analysis. To reach into these real meanings of African American women's lives and experience becomes the kind of tapping power — that power that can be held among African American women — in which womanist theologians and ethicists participate. Womanist theology aims to develop from African American women's life experiences as one of its basic sources. The foundational experiences of tapping power, engaging an embodied spirituality that can lead to change, can provide a way to tap into African American women's life meanings. The following four chapters look more closely at the rich textures of African American women's healing, health, and spirituality, in a variety of places and in various ways.

TWO

Mamas and Aunties

Roles and relationships are a source for African American women's tapping power. In the roles that African American women adopt in their homes and communities, power is often initiated. The relationships themselves are symbolic of healing in African American communities: mama, granny, auntie, and girlfriend. The relationships imply acts of healing individuals or communities through nurture. Beginning the exploration of the meanings of tapping power, this chapter investigates the complex shapes of African American mamas and aunties, sometimes looking back at history in order to understand present roles.

Mamas

*Religiosity is the guise [used to keep black people out of power].
. . . I remember so clearly, as a child, being told by a woman,
"Wearing lipstick is a sin and you wouldn't want Jesus to come
back right now and see you," and we had just left our mothers,
putting on lipstick.* — Lisa, interviewed in Detroit, 1996

Mothering is a conflicted role for African American women who are bombarded with mixed messages. There are too few mentors and fewer community supports at the same time as the upwardly mobile struggles increase. As mothers, African American women are often negatively perceived by the general public — unmarried, uncaring, ignorant, or incapable. The story of Tabitha Walrond in New York, an African American unmarried mother, serves as an example.

On a doctor's advice, Tabitha Walrond had breast reduction surgery at the age of fifteen. Tabitha became pregnant in high school and gave birth at age nineteen, two days before her graduation. When she had her son, again taking medical advice, Tabitha decided to breast feed. While she was in prenatal and postpartum care, none of her medical staff considered her previous breast reduction. As she tried to feed her child, Tabitha knew something was wrong and had taken her son to an outpatient clinic. But because her Medicaid card had not yet arrived, she was turned away. Her son died of malnutrition at the age of two months.

The case generated a storm of publicity. Negative interpretations of Tabitha came through in newspaper accountings of the case.

[Robert] Holdman had argued in his opening statement that Ms. Walrond deliberately let her child starve because she was angry at his father, Keenan Purrell, who had broken up with her and gotten another woman pregnant. . . . At a press conference after the verdict, Robert T. Johnson, the Bronx District Attorney, was critical of the demonstrators who protested the prosecution. "It's not a breast-feeding issue when the baby's dying," he said, pointing to testimony by the baby's father that he had urged Ms. Walrond to feed her son formula eight days before his death. "This case was about her failure to get help for a two-month-old baby who was starving over the course of his life. . . . It was clear that the baby didn't get like that in a minute. How can you imagine any mother seeing her child like that and not absolutely jumping up and down in the emergency room saying, 'Look at my child'? . . . " In his summation, Mr. Holdman ridiculed the defense medical experts, saying of the defendant, "She could bring experts in from all over the country, but she couldn't go a couple of blocks to a clinic?"[1]

In these comments, it is clear that the perception of fault in the infant's death was easily placed on the black, inadequate mother and not the system.

Tabitha's attorney, Susan Tipograph, stated in a phone conversation in 2002, "Every conceivable system that should have been for her, failed her. But who got blamed?" As her case received press, more and more public outrage surfaced. Of the nine hundred letters that the courts received, most were from middle-class white women who had similar physical challenges to mothering; these women had the income and health care resources to receive better advice, including, when deemed necessary, lactation counselors. Tabitha had had no such options. She had had, however, enough public outcries to keep her case from the invisibility that most African American mothers on trial would have experienced. Tabitha, charged with the lesser offense of criminally negligent homicide, was convicted in May 1999 and received a sentence of five years' probation.

Being black and a woman in the United States warrants minimal respect at best. Gender, race, and class intertwine to shape multifaceted, multilayered oppressions. As one aspect of these oppressions, gender is no protection from male assault and insult, no matter how "ladylike" one acts. In fact, gender becomes the motivation for derogation of black women who, like black men, are suspected of multiple forms of sexual deviance that are race based: licentiousness, promiscuity, bestiality, or any form of self-indulgent behavior. "Sexual racism is an inherent problem in integrated cultures. It is a carefully orchestrated and integral part of the white man's control over his kingdom and therefore is unfortunately adopted by some black men as a de facto part of American culture."[2] Only processes of desexualizing African American women are proof against suspicion; the stereotype of "mammy" is one such unsexed and safe black figure. Notwithstanding their denigrated image as women, they get even less respect as mothers.

The bottom line for African American women in mothering roles: take care of everybody but yourself and don't expect praise for it. The tasks of teaching their children how to survive in a world that does not care for them fall to black mothers. These lessons have been integral to the lives of African Americans. During enslavement, as historian Walter Johnson pointed out, there was a process of "shaping" the enslaved Africans' bodies to slavery.[3] Physical violence, threats of violence, and the constant menace of being sold and sent far away were part of daily life. Enslaved mothers lived under an intimidating cloud, as they found ways to prepare their children for eventual whippings at the hand of the master. Black feminist and critical theorist Angela Davis cites two different versions of a lullaby, one version sung to white babies:

> Hushaby,
> Don't you cry
> Go to sleep, little baby.
> And when you wake,
> You shall have a cake
> And all the pretty little ponies.

However, the following version was sung to black children who were being shaped for slavery.

> Go to sleep, little baby,
> When you wake
> You shall have
> All the mulies in the stable.
> Buzzards and flies
> Picking out its eyes,
> Poor little baby crying,
> Mamma, mamma![4]

As stated in the previous chapter, the illusion was that all oppressive experiences ended with the Emancipation Proclamation and enslavement was abolished. However, the processes of colonizing mothers and their children, of shaping bodies to new or revised constraints, continue. For instance, how do today's African American mothers teach their children to *drive while black*? When only a small percentage of African Americans have college degrees, how do black women guide their children through educational systems from which they are distanced? How do women communicate to their children anything about a world from which they have been excluded? Clearly, the problems are not over. The film documentary by Jennifer Dworkin, *Love and Diane*, traced three generations of poor African American women in New York City over a five-year period.

The film depicted three generations of black women battered by poverty, poor education, unemployment, pregnancies, and substance abuse. *Love and Diane* superbly presented stark pictures of the daily realities and limited choices of poor African American women.

In spite of the challenges that black women face in mothering, American society's views generally remain negative. "American culture reveres no Black Madonna, it upholds no popular image of a Black mother nurturing her child."[5] During the 1990s and the political campaigns to end "handouts" for the "unworthy," the welfare mother was often painted as black, licentious, and wallowing in undeserved benefits from her incessant self-gratifying behaviors. Drug usage, with crack cocaine in particular, was seen as an extension of this stereotypical African American mother's self-indulgence pattern. With the brutal governmental budget *slash-and-burn* tactics for Americans in need, welfare is now considered reformed. But poor women and their children are still here. However, as two researchers stated in 2002: "The result has been that America entered its most recent recession as defenseless as if we had to face a terrorist attack without firefighters or emergency rescue workers. The safety net that sustained millions of the poor through previous downturns, however inadequately, has been torn to shreds."[6]

Regardless, the attacks on black mothers through popular American images have not ended, and the tragedies are constantly overlooked. Variations on the theme of "bad black mother" keep the negative images alive. White America shakes their heads regarding black teenage mothers. The implication is that these girls are a source of the failure of African Americans to pull themselves up by nonexistent bootstraps. Anthropologist Brett Williams sharply analyzed this injustice:

> The "reproductive underclass" and its icon, the teen mother, thus conflate social class with ideas about time within a class-appropriate life course. Her inability to defer gratification and her subsequent lifelong imputed dependency on the government make her responsible for her poverty, a reproductive

threat to the rest of us, and the antithesis of the proper citizen worker who produces goods and services rather than babies.[7]

Another variation on the same theme is that the black single mother is the source of all evils. This resurrected variation had notably surfaced in the late 1960s under discussions of a castrating "black matriarchy" as the root of evil. Daniel Moynihan, prior to becoming a U.S. senator from New York, wrote *The Negro Family: A Case for National Action* in 1965. Womanist ethicist Traci West notes that Moynihan

> argued that black women's role in black families was respon-
> sible for disadvantaging the race. Under the chapter heading
> "The Tangle of Pathology," Moynihan reported that the "ma-
> triarchial structure" of the Negro family seriously retards the
> progress of the group as a whole, and imposes a crushing bur-
> den on the Negro male and, in consequence, on a great many
> Negro women as well. Because too many black families are
> headed by single moms they are "pathological" and spell doom
> for the progress of the race.[8]

For the twenty-first century, there are new twists to an old line of argument.

The birth rate for unmarried African American women in 2000 was 72.5 per 1000 unmarried black women, the number second highest after Hispanic women.[9] But the rate alone does not tell the story. The U.S. Census Bureau reported that single-mother families increased to 2 million among total families of all races in the year 2000. That number is much greater among African Americans, with approximately 47 percent of black family groups headed by women.[10] Families headed by women, compared to those headed by men, are more likely to have more than one child. In general, women-headed households are more likely to have poverty-level incomes. As a further distancing from resources, African American women are less likely to have been married in these families, so there is less likelihood of economic support from the birth fathers.[11]

These women-headed households are significant in relationship to the health care industry. African American women who have no fiscal resources to obtain health care often end up using emergency rooms as the most regular medical care. While some state-funded programs provide limited health care for the children of single parents, they usually exclude regular care for the parent. However, these facts are seldom considered when blame is placed at the door of the women who have no men in the household to provide additional (imagined) economic resources. An example of the blame game came up at a conference in a question asked by a male internist. He spoke with a heavy first-generation accent. The anger in his tone may have somewhat strengthened his accent as he asked, "Why *don't* black women stay with their men?" His analysis was implied in his question: the women were at fault for leaving the men. The guilt for poverty, poor health care, risky child rearing, and family destruction are laid at the feet of the African American single mother.

Returning to Tabitha Walrond for a moment: she received her associates' degree in 2003 and was making plans to continue her education to obtain her bachelor's degree. Her story became known, and because of this, she received some support. But had she not had that support, she would have been one more statistic used as the cause for the failure of American society. African American women have to consciously work to find healing from the harmful effects of being black and female and usually poor in the United States.

African American Mothers and Healing

I don't want to be negative [laughs] but . . . that's where internal healing comes in, because you have to find a way to work and proceed in this world, know who you are, and know that the change is so gradual, so gradual, it probably won't happen in your lifetime.   —MELODY, interviewed in Detroit, 1997

In the midst of external societal realities, mothering takes place in African American communities. Black feminist Carol Boyce Davies drew from literature by black women to discuss the healing aspects of mothering:

> Mothering and healing are intricately connected and of central thematic importance. . . . Reflecting a distinctly Black feminist point of view, these writers reveal that Black women, at certain junctures in their lives, require healing and renewal and that Black women themselves have to become the healers/mothers for each other when there is such a need. The recurring theme of mothering communicates the important message that survival alone and persistent mothering of others cannot be considered sufficient. . . . [12]

Mothering among African American women is reciprocal, emphasizing women's responsibilities and possibilities. "Significantly, much of this mothering is directed at releasing the inner self being suffocated by race and sex oppression."[13] Mothering functions to fashion networks of women who significantly contribute in the creation of black identities and communities.

The views of mothers from within African American communities, however, are not always aligned with the negative images presented in the white American mind. One significant reason this distinction in views remains is the continued division between black and white Americans. The separation of races in the United States afforded African Americans the opportunity to retain their own understandings, derived from African cultural orientations. The language of "orientations" was developed by Sidney Mintz and Richard Price, conceptualizing how African American cultures developed. They posit the idea that African cognitive orientations were part of the mentalities of those brought to America as slaves. These orientations were

> basic assumptions about social relations (which values motivate individuals, how one deals with others in social situations, and matters of interpersonal style), and . . . basic assumptions and expectations about the way the world functions phenomenologically (for instance, beliefs about causality, and

how particular causes are revealed). We would argue that certain common orientations to reality may tend to focus the attention of individuals from West and Central African cultures upon similar kinds of events, even though the ways for handling these events may seem quite diverse in formal terms.[14]

The trans-African/American similarities are manifest when African societies are visited today. Sylvia Ardyn Boone studied the society of women in one African community in Sierra Leone. Boone's journey into the Sande Society of the Mende people is an example of the close relationships with the cognitive orientations of African Americans.

The Sande women are initiated into a society that teaches the young girls what it means and how to be women. Men are initiated into a different but separate society. The passage to womanhood is learning the secrets of women and being criticized by the wise women for failing to measure up to the standards. The process teaches the philosophy and ethics of the entire community. Aesthetically, beauty is found in people, but especially in women. Boone noted one of the folk sayings that reflect this thinking: "Woman is the most beautiful thing that God has put in the world; she is God's finest handiwork."[15] In Mende aesthetics, a beautiful woman is shaped from childhood, learning social behaviors and bodily care. In this view, the beautiful woman is expected to be plumper than a man. Of note is the appreciation given to buttocks' "size, shape and movement." Women with small or flat behinds are derided: "Your behind is as flat as a winnowing fan."[16] However, to be beautiful is not enough: you must also be useful.

> Mende call this *nyande gbama,* empty beauty, *gbama* meaning "for nothing, in vain...." It is *gbama* for a good-looking girl to be rude, insolent, disrespectful. It is *gbama* for her to be nonfunctional in the community: "She can't work, can't cook, can't dance, can't sing — of what use is she?" It is *gbama* to be poor, of low status, living in coarse company.... It is beauty wasted.... Certainly the most serious *gbama* is barrenness.[17]

There is a kind of cruel irony in this brief glimpse into Boone's study. African American women seldom have such a positive, communally shared view of their beauty. Certainly, childbearing by African American women is seldom applauded by larger society as a sign of beauty.

African American women have developed cultural understandings of mothering that borrow from, and are built on, remnants of African cognitive orientations. Patricia Hill Collins refers to motherhood in the black communities as an institution in itself. "Motherhood can serve as a site where Black women express and learn the power of self-definition, the importance of valuing and respecting ourselves, the necessity of self-reliance and independence, and a belief in Black women's empowerment."[18]

Studies in different fields are beginning to recognize that the academic, diagnostic models derived from European cultural frameworks may not be appropriate for all people. In her significant research in social work, Joyce West Stevens drew some important conclusions about African American women as mothers and as daughters. Stevens proposes that there are four dimensions to parenting children to withstand racial injustices: "concrete experience as a criterion of meaning... the use of dialogue in assessing knowledge claims... the ethic of caring... [and] the ethic of personal accountability."[19] The centrality of the mother figure in imparting wisdom is critical. The information is, at its base, healing: knowledge that *you* are of value in a world that seeks to deny it will most likely be achieved if someone believes in you and in your value.

Stevens boldly asks if, considering that poor black girls are more often reared in single-parent homes, "Is the mother-daughter relationship among economically disadvantaged girls developmentally more critical than that of their more privileged cohorts?" The question exposes the painful reality of being poor, black, and female. Stevens states unequivocally: "Ultimately, African American female adolescents learn the race, ethnic, and gender role commitment by means of the intersubjective connections of the mother-daughter relationship."[20]

Additionally, Stevens notes that there are other socialization tasks that are performed by African American parents or caregivers for all the children under their care: "(1) keeping children safe (physically and emotionally) from the dangers of street life, (2) protecting children from overt forms of racism and oppression, and (3) helping children develop bicultural competence."[21]

The stressful role of fulfilling multiple commitments, especially for poor mothers, is daunting. They are often required to pass on information they do not have. Setting firm boundaries has often been one way that mothers have tried to pass on information and mold their children. Black mothers often attempt to heal by setting limits. Some of the sayings of African American mothers are clues for ceasing a certain behavior: "Mama don't play that" or "I'm not having that in my house." Some limits are set with unequivocally strong statements: "I brought you into this world, I'll take you out" or "I'm not scared of anything that came out of my body." Inappropriate behavior by children or acting out in public was tantamount to sacrilege. At other times, "The Look" that black mothers can give is a signal to control behavior, and is more than a cut of the eyes but will involve head, neck, and hands on hips.

Black mothers often exhibit the desired behavior to their children by their behavior toward their own mothers. In African American families, the grandmother role is no mere cookie-baking lady, but often a powerful figure in her own right. It is not unusual for a grandmother to be referred to as "Big Mama," indicating her significant position and role in the life of the family.

The influence of an African American grandmother is told by Joanne Braxton. The grandmother significantly connected the past to the present, while influencing the future of the grandchild.

> I thought Grandma would live forever, and it was a shock to me when she died three years ago. My grandmother was an artist. She was a celebrated cook, as her mother before her had been...now, my grandmother was also what I call a griotte, an Afra-American version of the griot, someone who transmits family history and traditions from generation to generation by

word of mouth. She was also a poet with an unparalleled love of language. I tell my students that when I can write poetry the way my grandmother could pray, I will be a real poet.[22]

I interviewed Mrs. Essie, mother of seven children, who was 103 years old at the time of our meeting. She told of her experiences as a mother, staying at home with the children. The family traveled from the South to the North in stages, and Mrs. Essie cared for the children, sometimes when her husband was with her and sometimes when she was alone and he was working out of town. She

> cooked what I could find to cook . . . I was off the welfare . . . I didn't have anything but I kept them clean with Goodwill stuff. . . . [My husband] was working at Ford's making five dollars a day with all those children. Every penny he earned, they'd take all of it, and that five dollars was gone! . . . If you tell [the children] something or another, you got to mean that. You have to put your foot down to let them know that you are the parent and they are the children. . . . You have to let them know if they didn't mind, that there were nice little switches out there. I'd get them and tear their legs up, and those little switches would make you mind! (Mrs. Essie, interviewed in Detroit, 2003)

But today, Mrs. Essie sees a break with the past. Parents no longer listen to the wisdom of older people, and community concern is broken. "They don't want no older people to interfere with them. . . . And so the only thing is to mind their own business. It's a lot going on that they don't know about."

Mrs. Essie's words indicate some of the shifts in the African American communities across the country, flagging community strength while continuing social problems must be faced. Whether her child-rearing practices were correct or not, they worked for the times of legal segregation and migration to urban centers. Her life experiences coupled with the mothers' sayings underline Stevens's three levels of socialization: keeping children safe, dealing with racism, and developing bicultural competencies. But the range of cultural competencies has grown and become a new set of challenges for African American mothers today. Continued economic hardships coupled with educational shut-outs make an already impossible situation even more impossible. Yet these challenges will not be the first that African American women, in their mothering roles, have undertaken.

In the role of mother, African American women learn prayer, deep prayer. How else are children raised or families nurtured? An activist sense of prayer informs many Christian black women's lives: activist because prayer is not a passive event, but a partnership with God. God is in the middle of each everyday moment, not contained in a church or confined to an hour of the week. God may speak through others, "angels," or through signs. But God surely speaks. God becomes a source of power to tap into; God is also a catalyst to help women discover their own power. A saying among African American women who have exhausted their own efforts to solve a certain problem references a kind of division of labor: "Take it to the feet of God — and leave it there. Don't go back and pick it up again."

Prayer is, first of all, a conversation, even when some formulae are used. Such a sense of prayer is part of the socialization of most black people, especially among African American women. Woven into quilts, kneaded into bread, or arranged in the furniture the presence of God is a source of information that floods African American women's lives. The Western mind-set that compartmentalizes "God in this corner" is alien to black cultural frameworks. It is a distinctive feature to African American spirituality: spirit and flesh are not in competition and God/Spirit works through all of it. While much Western theology gives voice to the concepts of the omnipotence and omnipresence of God, African American spirituality lives the wonder of God's presence and activity. It is so much a part of our lives that we tend to take it for granted. A few examples will clarify.

Womanist ethicist Traci West researched African American women and sexual violence. She noted how two of her informants recognized God's presence in violent situations. "The combination of both accounts provides texture and detail for a theology that acknowledges God's active presence during and after male sexual assault. Women recognize divine power as definitively located on their side. God intercedes on their behalf. In one instance God ensures, in the other God can be depended upon to bring justice."[23] African American women across the economic spectrum acknowledge the sense of God's activity in their lives. Patti LaBelle was a well-established performer during the time she wrote of learning of her mother's death: "God sent me an angel to tell me my mother died. I guess He knew that was the only way I could take it."[24] Or as she reflected with another famous singer, Cindy Birdsong, on having a successful career: "Cindy, who has dedicated her life to the Lord, said that God was using me to spread a message.... I know what I do is blessed or God wouldn't have left me here to carry on."[25] These ideas of prayer as action-oriented, linked to survival and justice, and defining life's meaning are normative for many African American women. Prayer is a tool for living, and black mothers use it liberally.

Combating Oppression from Home

This chapter is not to lionize African American women as mothers; there is no guarantee that all African American women are a nurturing source for their children. The potential for failure because of struggles against social limitations and oppressive situations is ever present. The pursuit of safety for children and family is one example. Some mothers have been known to limit their children's activities to the extent that affords no possibility of growth. Another form of overprotection is when mothers refuse to let children participate in anything that is beyond the mothers' scope of knowledge. The logic supporting these actions is: if the children do not get involved in the unknown, the chances of hurt are lessened. Many African American parents stress the importance of education, but have no idea how to prepare a child for higher education. A desire to travel or to make money or to become successful sounds exciting when parents think of their children's potential; but when parents have no clue how to lead a child to those opportunities, these can become dreams that frustrate parents and offspring.

Any group of parents in the United States can state their desire to keep children safe, yet it becomes a critical issue in black communities. How can African American children's safety be assured when the parents or guardians work longer for less money? How can African American children's futures be assured when educational opportunities are reduced to testing results between unequal systems? When black families have fewer external resources — no Uncle Joe with a summer job to give or a time share to lend — how are they expected to compete as the haves continue to outdistance them? The ongoing affirmative action of white privilege is a reality in America and batters black families. African American parents' desire to keep children safe is not new and is woven into a brutal history. Today, however, educational systems in urban education centers have few, if any, methods to address the shortfall of parental knowledge and no systematic ways to offer support to single mothers. The educational systems, which are stressed with their own burdens, often fall back on blaming the bad single mothers who don't show up for parent nights. This ignores the reality that protection without resources is often limited to keeping children close to home as long as possible.

Related to the ideas of protecting children, another pitfall for African American mothers is the myth of the need to "raise daughters and love sons." It springs from the belief that African American women have an easier time, educationally and economically, in U.S. society, and therefore, black girls need less nurturing than boys. A saying in African American communities enforces the myth: "The only two free creatures in America are white men and black women." Thus, sons need more care than daughters. As a result, daughters are often set up to be caregivers for the male children. The myth of the ease of black female success exists in African American communities in various forms and can become one part of the problem between black men and women that need healing or are healing, as discussed in greater detail in chapter 4.

Being able to reunite with African/African American connections through the availability of travel and information about Africa, as in Sylvia Ardyn Boone's book, has made it easier for African American women to find links to positive views of themselves and of motherhood. For example, some African American women have experienced rites of passage, Americanized versions reflecting new realities but still containing the values that the Sande or other African societies have. Mary C. Lewis developed a program for rites of passage specific to adolescent girls that includes focus on current female issues. Lewis's material was compiled from research done on adolescent development, African American life conditions, and cultural perspectives, and incorporates the Nguzo Saba, or seven principles of Blackness that were established in the mid-1960s by African Americans.[26] Some of the programs of rites of passage are offered under the auspices of black churches. But some women find sources on their own, because there is such an interest in healing negative social views of being black and female in America, which are compounded by views of black motherhood.

Some black American women return to Africa to participate in rites of passage. In a book about African American women's travels, Adrienne Johnson described her adult participation with her mother:

> My mother was first. We had just left a dark room to sit in a row of stools in the center of the Ghanaian town of Aku-tukope. We had received wisdom from elders, been wrapped in fine handwoven cloth, and adorned in strands of beads culled from the earth. And now, amid the noise of celebration, the head of the village — a woman — guided my mother in front of a man with a short black sword.... The crowd cheered. My mother was being embraced by these people. And she was being renamed. Bea Johnson was now Queen Mother Amertoryor.[27]

The relationships between African and African American women can become a source of healing, especially as we view ourselves as mothers and as women, coming to understand why our views of gender and gendered relationships are distinct. African American women have lived in separate societies from white American women. White American women stress lack of recognition from their male counterparts who hoard the social power. But gender difference generally functioned another way for African American women and men, so justice from black American women's perspectives seldom matches the view that white women have. This is one important reason that feminism has been an uncomfortable concept for many African American women.

Additionally the ways that African American women view themselves often resonate with many aspects of African women, particularly in shared values. As some African American women read Boone's book, for example, the surprised comment often surfaces: "I wondered where this or that idea came from in the African American community — and here it is!" Loosely paralleling some African social structures (of which Boone's is one example), single-sex groupings have been part of African American life. This is notable in the structures of some American black churches as womanist sociologist Cheryl Townsend Gilkes notes:

> Recent observations and comparative analyses of contemporary African and black American church traditions have acknowledged a parallel between the prayer leadership of black women in all variations of black Protestantism and the African Queen Mother and between the distinctive role of black pastors' wives and African female leadership. In addition, the roles to which the labels "teacher," "missionary," "evangelist," and "deaconess" are affixed are wide-ranging in their rights, duties, obligations, authority and structural relationships within a congregation or a denomination.[28]

These are examples of what Gilkes terms "dual-sex politics," which have African roots and form differences from white American cultures. Some of the differences are seen in the discussion of church mothers who, among others, are examples of African American women taking mothering into the community.

Mothers of the Community

Drawing from African cognitive frameworks, mothering includes both birth mothers and other black women of the communities. In other words, the concept of mothering is not restricted to biological functions. Mothering, from a black perspective, is better described as a state of spirit rather than of the body. There is security for one black mother who is confident that other black women are there to help. One result of the mothering concept is, as black feminist sociologist Patricia Hill Collins stated, "organized, resilient, women-centered networks of blood mothers and African Americans."[29] The communal "African American" aspect of the black women's institution of motherhood also serves a healing function. The African American role is not limited to those women with blood ties to a child. Community members might step in to arrange for a child's care when the mother is absent. Karen Baker-Fletcher, a womanist theologian, highlights an example.

> Such extended family patterns until very recently were normative in African American culture. There are stories of schoolteachers known for truly loving children, sometimes collecting children's clothes and giving them to children from families in financial difficulty. Such teachers take time to get to know the children and their families, becoming part of their lives, not charity workers. There are teachers who have combed a student's hair in the morning because her mother was not able to. Such women are "other mothers."[30]

It is ironic that in the past few years some people critique the black community as weakened because informal other mothering is less frequent; women might no longer step forward to pick up abandoned children. The irony is that legislation has no method of recognizing the other mothering role and has curtailed many possibilities. By law, a child must be enrolled in school and must have shots and a birth certificate. The person who is responsible for the child must be a legal guardian. In order to become a legal

guardian, court proceedings consume time and money, and the proposed guardian's life must be examined. The guardian's role must
be clarified: is this an adoption? Even African American grand-
parents who end up with care for the next generation must answer
this question. Adoption then formally ends the birth parents' role;
this is sometimes necessary, but most often in black communities, the birthmother and other mothers work together for a child's
benefit. The other legal option, foster care, is its own nightmare,
where African American children may be lost in an overburdened,
underfunded system. Other mothering is an informal networking
system that builds community and ensures a child's protection by a
network of adults. "Today, even when flesh-and-blood family is not
present, many Black Americans form networks with 'fictive kin.'
While the extended family has received some wear and tear, it has
not died out."[31]

Many black churches continue to hold healthy extended family connections and to provide settings in which African American
women exercise a mothering authority. Through prayer activities
and support in the challenges and changes of life, the church can
become a therapeutic setting, a location of safety where African
American women can freely express themselves.[32]

An important expression of the mothering role is that of the
church mother. The role may be formal or informal in a church
setting, but the importance of church mothers is clear.

> In almost all cases, she is an older woman, often elderly, who
> is considered an example of spiritual maturity and morality to
> the rest of her congregation. Her career as a Christian is usu-
> ally exemplary and long... she is one of the few people whose
> seat in the congregation is formally or informally reserved.
> When she dies, her seat may be draped in black.[33]

Her role is not merely honorary, but serves a healing function in
the congregation. She may function formally or informally and
her responsibilities can include settling disputes, correcting adults
and children, holding members of the congregation in prayer, and
reminding all members of the conditions of the church covenant.

The nurturing by church mothers, other mothers, and birth mothers are examples of healing by African American women. These processes of nurture are often in defiance of a world that threatens to destroy them; many of these women have seemingly nonexistent resources to combat such forces. For many African American women, these processes are grounded in faith in a God who never fails, is a sure partner, and becomes a center of hope in hopeless situations. Grounded in African cognitive orientations, their sense of nurturing is not merely for the individual's good but for the benefit of the community, or as the African proverb states, "I am because we are." Other mothers and church mothers are primary examples of the nonindividualistic view of being a mother. Mothering extends into the shaping of community.

The shaping of community is an indication of African American women's agency to achieve healing and wholeness, regardless of the attempts of dominant society to create unhealthy boundaries. Darlene Clark Hine, in her research as a historian, wrote of the communal dimension of black women's work.

> Black women created essential new communities and erected vast female networks during the transitions from slavery to freedom, from farm to city. It was through "making community" that Black women were able to redefine themselves, project sexual respectability, reshape morality, and define a new aesthetic.[34]

African American women's caring for the health of the community derived from their African understandings of healing and personal power and was refined during enslavement in interaction with and on behalf of the community.[35] This care for the community health did not end with the Emancipation Proclamation but continued to be a vital part of life in black communities. This dimension of community-building is seen repeatedly in African American women's efforts to care for the health of the community and is the focus of chapter 6. The remainder of this chapter is for another role of black women closely allied with mothering, and that is auntie.

Aunties and Healing

We are a magical force. Magic is the energy we create with un-
conditional love, and that is a powerful creative force. It's not
leaving it to something out there, because spirit is in here. It's
surrounding us, it's in us ... it's what makes us strong when
we're not supposed to be here anymore.
                    — LISA, interviewed in Detroit, 1996

An African American woman might receive the designation of
"auntie" in her relationships with a certain household. This is
also a nurturing role with potential for healing disputes in that
family. The role often happens when a friendship grows with the
mother/female guardian, but this is not always the case. "Auntie"
has authority to speak in a given household, sometimes in a given
situation. The woman called "Auntie" may have some expertise to
share, and that is when she is called upon to speak. In other words,
Auntie has some formal mentoring role within a family setting. I
was in my late teens before I found out that "Auntie so and so"
really was not related by blood. But God help me if I ever decided
not to follow her directions. Her word had authority and weight in
my family; she was accepted at all gatherings and was expected to
show up for graduations and funerals. If other mothering is per-
plexing to people who do not understand these cultural operations
of "fictive kin," then the auntie is even more baffling.

I bring Auntie into the picture to demonstrate the complexities
of roles and the possibilities of women healing in African American communities. Mothers, other mothers, and church mothers are
not the only ways that black women use relationships to provide
links that hold community together. The positive energy to build
relationships is the energy that constitutes communities. This is
healing: community battles the isolation of individualism. I am
not claiming that African American communities are perfect. However, the webbing of relationships is critical for survival. There are
many forms of family that are unrecognized outside of black communities. I believe that the existence of these relationships fuels
creativity: a people whom others attempted to "shape" for slavery

found ways to retain clan connections and personal identity. Some of those ways of retaining connections continue.

Auntie is a role that is one step removed from Mama. Auntie is the one to call to get a reading on how Mama might take some news. Or, in some situations, Auntie might be the one to call first to intercede with Mama. Aunties prove that African American family is not, as some pundits have claimed, dead.

My daughter is in her twenties now, independent, living away from home. I was complaining about something she was doing to a woman who is a longtime friend. The woman who has a daughter the same age as mine was mutually shocked. "I can't believe she is doing that. You bring her over here to Auntie when she gets back in town. I'll straighten her out." I dropped my daughter off at her house when she visited. I don't have any idea what was said, but it worked. There were no blood ties to constitute this "auntie" relationship. Rather it grew from mutual concern for nurturing children, even when those children are adults. Our friend's declaration of being Auntie was welcomed by both my daughter and me; it was, for us, a natural expression of our familial-like relationship. Auntie grows from a sense of sisters and friends, and the circle widens to extend into the community.

Auntie is an appropriate discussion within the wider conversation about black women and healing because it demonstrates a fluidity that creates community and heals by means of relationships. The flexibility of identifying family is a process of crossing lines that are deemed unimportant: who gave birth to whom is nearly an academic discussion. A more important knowledge is: who truly stands on my behalf, ultimately meaning that lines of birth and place are often crossed in order to construct *new* meaning.

Other lines that are crossed include those of time. An example is found in Lalita Tademy's account of her authorship of *Cane River*, a fictionalized story of the women in her family's history in Jim Crow Louisiana.[36] Tademy knew of the legends of the women in her family, had even received the written accounts of another family member. Although she had a successful corporate career, Tademy reported that she would often find herself daydreaming about the historic women in her family. "In 1995, driven by a hunger I could not name, I surprised myself and quit my job, walking away from a coveted position for which I had spent my life preparing."[37] Tademy began researching the women's history, and wrote of her sense of being in relationship with them:

> Emily's mother, Philomene, came to life before any of the others. She visited my dreams, urging me to tell their stories. No, "urging" is too tame a word, too remote. Philomene *demanded* that I struggle to understand the different generations of my family and the complexities of their lives. She made it unacceptable that any of them be reduced or forgotten. It defies description in words, this bond I have with Philomene and her ability to reach across four generations to me with such impact.[38]

Tademy's story makes sense within an African American epistemology, which is daily informed by a spirituality that connects the individual self in the present moment with those ancestors who have gone before. The consciousness of those earlier women and men who most likely sacrificed and suffered is found in the saying that "I stand on their shoulders": any successes of this present moment are only understood in connection with the people who sacrificed in an earlier time. For all I may have achieved in my life, I know that I have ancestors standing at my back, looking over my shoulder, and yes, sometimes interfering in my present moment. In a similar way, aunties come into relationship in the present moment, guarding, mentoring, and guiding. Another story of relationships and black women crosses the Atlantic and emphasizes the healing power that is tapped in claiming "auntie."

"Sarah Bartmann was a Khoekhoe woman, who was born in the southern Cape [South Africa] in 1788."[39] Yvette Abrahams is a womanist historian from Cape Town who began her doctoral thesis on Sarah Bartmann, also from the same clan. (The clan, Khoekhoe, has been misnamed by Europeans as "Hottentots.") However, Sarah Bartmann was enslaved by Hendrik Cezar and exhibited as a freak in England. Her genitalia were the prurient interest of Europeans who decreed her deviant. Later transferred to the new "owner-ship" of Mssr. Reaux (who exhibited wild animals) in Paris, Sarah Bartmann died in 1815. The interest in her continued: she was dismembered and her genitalia were displayed in museums. As one black feminist anthropologist noted, relating to views of all black women: "When Sarah Baartman (*sic*) was kidnapped for exhibition in Europe in the early nineteenth century, her body was placed at the unsavory intersection of slavery, an Enlightenment classificatory system, and quasi-pornographic notions of medicine. The Black woman's body was both an instrument of prurient fascination and a historical symbol of service-oriented labor."[40]

At the end of the twentieth century, Sarah Bartmann's remains were finally returned to her homeland, and Yvette Abrahams began the task of writing her Ph.D. thesis on Bartmann. Because Abrahams is from the same clan, she experienced great pain in trying to write about this lost ancestor. Abrahams could not distance herself from the connections between herself and Bartmann.

> You have to understand, in my culture, that there is simply no way for me to relate to a lady almost two centuries older than myself other than by treating her with extreme respect. If we had only had a passing acquaintance, I would have addressed her as "Mrs. Bartmann," but by this time we were meeting on a daily basis. So, although we are not blood relatives I should call her "auntie" and address her at all times in the third person.[41]

Abrahams contrasted her attitude with other written materials about Bartmann and makes a connection to her and other black women.

> This is still what it means to be auntie Sarah. After a hundred and eighty five years, her body is still lying on the table of countless [undergraduates] swotting for their courses in race and representation, literature, art history, history, anthropology or the history of medicine.... The social construction of racism and sexism has rendered the abuse which was performed against auntie Sarah Bartmann's body and her image

socially invisible to the perpetrators and, sometimes, to the victims. Instead, it has been represented as an ideologically innocuous activity. This academic violence has been state-subsidized and state-supported, represented as innocent by the mass media. In the process, it has rendered the violence done to other Black women, such as myself, invisible.[42]

Yvette Abrahams, in her story of relating with Sarah Bartmann and especially in her comparison with other dehumanizing views, presents a compelling demonstration of the healing power of Auntie. How do black women recognize our own worth in a world that continues to demean us? How can we pick up threads of a lost past? The healing process is a spiritual journey to retain what we have or recover from amputations. When we find ways to hold our connections with one another, we discover blessings in each other: holiness can be found in our families, no matter how they appear to others.

THREE

GRANNY MIDWIVES AND GIRLFRIENDS

What you supposed to do when they tell you you nobody?
You supposed to look in the mirror, embrace yourself, and say,
"Well, maybe you don't love me but God loves me." See, I re-
cently spent a lot of time with myself. . . . You know I'm not
the most educated person in the world, but not all educa-
tion is found in books. You can have good wisdom and good
spirituality for direction.

— MATTIE, interviewed in Detroit, 1997

Mothering and its forms are not the only ways that African American women create avenues toward wholeness. Chapter 3 moves into
other healing relationships in which African American women participate, past and present. The first section of the chapter discusses
granny midwives. The granny was a figure that dealt with one of the
most intimate parts of women's lives: birth. Some accounts of practicing granny midwives, including an interview with one woman
who is currently in practice, make up the second section of the
chapter.

The third section explores the concept of sister/friends. Giving
birth, for African American women, is more than a biological process; therefore the powerful healing work of girlfriends or sister/
friends is linked to that of the granny. This sister/friend role is one
that provides support among African American women as we attempt, like the grannies and the birth mothers, to develop our lives
in the face of the odds against us.

Granny Midwives: The Past

Under enslavement black people's bodies became subjected to white colonization. Black women were viewed through the European aesthetic lens that deemed their bodies shameful even while they were considered sexually available. During the period of enslavement and continuing through the long years of Jim Crow, many white people continued to believe that disrespecting the very humanity of black people was correct behavior. Health care for black people was not the same as that offered white people. Black women learned ways to hold on to their humanity and to resist the attempted control of their bodies. Health care became an arena where black women learned to exert their power, becoming agents who acted in their own interests. These expressions were sometimes in contrast to the "healthful" help that was given by white people.

An example of this conflict is noted in Marie Jenkins Schwartz's research on breast-feeding practices during enslavement. The care of black infants had different meanings to enslaved black people than it did to those who claimed to own them. The enslaved mother was caring for her child; the owner was caring for barely human "stock." Schwartz recounts a method that was published in a leading antebellum agricultural journal as a lockjaw preventative.

> One physician and planter recommended that owners withhold mother's milk for the first ten days of a slave baby's life, substituting as nourishment "sweet oil and molasses in such proportions as will keep the bowels loose." During this time the mother's milk was to be drawn off by the nurse, the midwife, another and older child or by a puppy.

Needless to say, the enslaved women did not follow these prescriptions. "The woman charged with supervising the plan's implementation apparently appropriated much of the oil and molasses for her own use."[1]

Although this is only one example of breast-feeding practices, it draws attention to underlying themes in the relationships between enslaved Africans and the dominant society's medical practices.

Black women and men were not considered human, legally counted as three-fifths human only for the sake of appropriating congressional seats for a state or determining the wealth of the purported owner. Like other stock or investment, the care of black bodies was important for income growth but never to the degree of draining the coffers. Therefore health care decisions for the enslaved were linked to concerns for the owners' profits and beliefs in the inhumanity of black people. However, the social and economic gulf between black and white also meant that white people were minimally exposed to the currents of black cultures. As a result, black people were often able to attend in their ways to their own physical care — certainly not with the resources of those in power, but drawing from other sources.

Utilizing their culturally based cognitive orientations, black people developed and maintained their own health practices. At the same time, black people learned to have a healthy skepticism for and fear of the white medical establishment. The account of recommended breast-feeding practices is but one of many that underline a continuous lineage of inhumane health practices devised for African Americans. In caring for themselves, black people served as agents on their own behalf. It was a significant matter for the survival of the group that the people did exercise their own agency.

In spite of the disparity, enslaved women's agency for the care of their communities drew from their own knowledge base. Ultimately, these women's health practices were foundational in the development of the white medical establishment. As one author pointed out:

That the daughters of Africa were a rich source of medical knowledge was not lost on the professional doctors of the Slave South, whose livelihood came from tending sick slaves. In an era when bleeding and purging were the medical profession's accepted therapies for most varieties of disease and conditions, doctors looked to these practicing slave women for information on how to cure the diseases of the slaves and those of their owners as well. . . . Once obtained, the medical news was rapidly disseminated throughout the newly organized medical community of the United States — in medical publications, in medical education and in meetings of fledgling professional associations of white medical men.[2]

The agency of African American women regarding health, healing practices, and care of their own bodies is illustrated by granny midwives. "To Negro women often fell another legally acceptable task: prenatal and obstetrical care of whites and blacks, especially in rural areas. Midwifery was an art."[3] Like other types of gender-defined work such as weaving, midwifery had the added potential to strengthen black women's networking. The importance of these networks of black women cannot be understated. As historian Deborah Gray White noted: "Strength had to be cultivated. It came no more naturally to them [black women] than to anyone, slave or free, male or female, black or white. If they seemed exceptionally strong it was partly because they often functioned in groups and derived strength from numbers."[4]

"Grannies" were usually older women who provided midwifery services and other doctoring, primarily for the other enslaved people, but sometimes also for white families. Womanist author Valerie Lee provides background on the development of the name.

> While older black women were "aunties," simply by virtue of a monolithic racial categorization, the grannies, as women too old for their masters' fields or sexual advances, at least enjoyed the distinction of a grouping by vocation. Sometimes called "cotton dollies," the grannies were not necessarily the same as the plantation's mammies. . . . The grannies, as if assured of their place in history, have themselves in past decades embraced "granny," not as a racial epithet, but as a derivative of *grand* — wise women who stand tall in their communities.[5]

In the shaping of the name "granny," another form of black women's agency on their own behalf is seen that countered the dehumanizing processes of shaping "slaves."

Birth for African American women was and is often an act of courage. Bringing children into a world that did not care for mother or child meant that other visions of their own humanity had to operate. African American women carried messages of other visions through informal networks, some of which were formalized, like the granny midwife. Granny midwives were afforded a great deal of autonomy because of their important roles in the birth process: to do so was, after all, a business decision on the part of the plantation owners. "Slave women in their late teens and early twenties were not free to consider their future without considering that their childbearing ability was of economic consequence to their owners. Since some masters figured that at least five to six percent of their profit would accrue from natural increase, this period in the bondswoman's life was beset with pressures that free women did not experience."[6] The midwives, then, had the role of ensuring the safe deliveries of the babies. The aid they provided in birthing processes was hampered by limited resources as they drew from herbal lore, common wisdom, and religious understandings. But the efficacy of their methods was not the sole basis from which they operated. Another important knowledge source for granny midwives was drawn from a cultural base, and they developed traditions based on "women-centered patterns" that were part of African cognitive orientations. In other words, the enslaved African women drew on their old knowledge in order to network; they functioned in a kind of underground self-help system. The grannies' role became more defined as they passed on the information.

The Midwife Traditions

The granny midwives continued working throughout the rural South after slavery formally ended. Black people still were not welcomed in the same hospitals that treated white people, and hospitals for black people were few. As long as most black people were in the South and in sharecropping situations, the granny was indispensable for her services. The grannies remained integral parts of the communities in which they worked, with what we would today term "holistic" understandings of health. "That the grannies were hesitant to divide their lives into categories of secular and sacred, traditional and orthodox, mind and body, modern and folk is no accident. They lived in communities that in various ways critiqued dualistic thinking."[7]

The midwives' responsibilities extended far beyond that of the actual birthing process; they also functioned as fertility, contraception, postpartum, nutrition, and pediatric advisors. One woman who was attended by a midwife in the 1940s stressed the differences: "Granny midwives did more caring. . . . There was more hands on, they touched you and made you feel [safe]. Yes, she would be sitting right there by your side, you wouldn't have a hard time like we do in the hospital, you hurting and nobody there to touch you."[8]

The grannies did whatever was necessary in the birth process and in subsequent infant care, including domestic chores and training the family members. "When I went to a home after delivery I would carry whatever they needed back. Food, soap, sheets, clothin that I could make. I would sit down a lot a days and just make not only the lil baby somethin to put on, the other babies too. . . . A lot of em was hungry."[9]

Since the nineteenth century, the medical profession became more established and the work of birthing was seen as part of obstetrics. "With the incorporation of forceps, anesthetic agents, and surgical procedures by the medical profession, the grannies' practices were increasingly viewed as mystical, rudimentary, and obsolete."[10] Granny midwives were slowly replaced by doctors and nurses using the legal system. A part of the legalization and control was that the grannies had to be licensed under state laws to operate as midwives, with the understanding that they were under the direction of a medical doctor. However, the shortage of physicians who would care for black women in their communities, particularly for childbirth, only served to delay the total replacement of grannies in African American communities. But the suppression of these granny midwives did occur.

The tensions between the legalized system of medicine and the practices of the grannies can be sensed from the words of the granny midwives. The words that follow are from three granny midwives: Onnie Lee Logan, Margaret Charles Smith, and Mama Leslie. Two worked during the same time period and the same state of Alabama. Alabama passed a law to place midwifery under the board of health in 1919. "The South was decades behind the rest of the country in establishing obstetrics for the care of all childbearing women. Midwifery became a Southern black phenomenon, and the South became the repository of the so-called midwife problem in America."[11] Both Onnie Lee Logan and Margaret Charles Smith had similar experiences: "instruction from public health nurses; were given written examinations; were subjected to monthly inspections of their equipment bags, their person, and their homes . . . and were expected to comply with all the stipulations."[12]

Onnie Lee Logan was born around 1910 and was a granny midwife in Alabama from 1949 until the practice was outlawed in 1976. Throughout her oral history, Logan identifies something critically important about her work that is heard again and again in the stories of granny midwives. The work of "baby catching" was identified as a calling from God, a spiritual gift, a vocation, incorporating remnants of African concepts of the spiritual dimensions of healing. "I do believe and know that there is a higher power. And He certainly will direct yo' path if you let Him. If you will trust Him, if you will serve Him, He will direct yo' path. He's not gonna let you make a mistake as long as you're workin in His name."[13]

There are tensions between childbirth from the faith-driven position and from the legalized medical community's science-driven position. The very sense of vocation and commitment to the community that the granny midwives knew creates the primary source of tension. Onnie Lee Logan knew her community: "During the first ten years of my career as a midwife, it was mainly black families I delivered for. Those black families . . . was po'. . . . Hardly nothing but po' in those days. It was po' times."[14] However, her attitude seldom condemned the people of the community and often attempted to help. She knew that she was preferable over the legalized medical doctor because "They was afraid, honey. . . . You know a long time ago black people were treated so dirty and so they was afraid of doctors givin em a dose of somethin just because they was black."[15] At the same time, her practices were centered on the natural approach: "Childbirth is not a sickness . . . I declare a woman gonna have a baby if she out there in the middle of the street. . . . Nobody supposed to pull that baby unless there is an emergency. . . . Her pressure and her own sense supposed to discard that baby from her body. The pressure from God."[16] In a like manner, Onnie Lee Logan placed God at the center of her own knowledge.

> There was a higher power and God give me wisdom. Motherwit, common sense. Wisdom come from on high. You got it and you cain't explain how you got it yo'self. It's motherwit. . . . It grew within my mind what to expect and what to think about. All at the same time God was talkin to me cause I was so interested. . . . But so many things I have run into that the classes did not teach me. . . . Two-thirds of what I know about deliverin, carin for mother and baby, what to expect, what was happenin and what was goin on, I didn't get it from class. God gave it to me. So many things I got from my own plain motherwit.[17]

Margaret Charles Smith was born in 1906 and began her career as a midwife in 1946. She attended her last birth in 1981. Mrs. Smith and her clients experienced the prejudice of the white medical establishment. "See, most of the doctors weren't too lovely with the colored folk. They had to make their money. . . . A lot of hospitals around here, they just wouldn't fool with you. The only place we had to carry a patient was to Tuskegee, and that was a long ways from here."[18]

From her own family, she remembered and respected black folkways of healing.

> The elder people back behind me had remedies that would help. People used to come to Mama for a lot of things. My grandmother used to give jimsonweed for fever. . . . When you are ready to have your baby, they used to give something like

bamboo briar that brings your pain on. . . . Mayapple root was good because if it wasn't your time for you to have a baby, it would stop those pains.[19]

She found ways to help a birthing mother's pain, including prayer. "You just keep a-talking to them until they finally make up in their mind that this is the only way. . . . Talk consolation. That's smart things. Some people have hard long labor, and you be standing by feeling sorry for them. You would say inside of your heart, 'Lord have mercy on this person.' "[20]

She is a longtime member of the Old Rehobeth Primitive Baptist Church, which she helped build, and she guessed there are about forty-five members of the church community. Margaret Charles Smith expresses a faith that radiates out to others eloquently. "Listen to me good now, when the Lord frees your soul, you can't hold it. You got to get out, if you don't do anymore than talk to the bushes and the posts and things. You don't have a private religion when the Lord frees your soul."[21]

Pregnancy and childbirth remain difficult for African American women. Prenatal care is important, but the distance that many black women feel from health care institutions may hamper positive health care. Mothering is risky from the time of conception.

As was true a century ago, our babies are still more than twice as likely to die before their first birthdays than those born to white women. This high infant mortality rate can in part be blamed on poverty, which keeps many women from getting adequate care when they are pregnant. But studies show that even Black middle-class women are more likely than white women of equal income and education levels to see their babies die.[22]

Some younger African American women attempt to continue the granny tradition. With the formality of legalized health care institutions today, these women are no longer called "grannies" but traditional midwives, distinguishing them from nurse midwives who work through hospitals. Mama Leslie is one of these.

Mama Leslie is African American and a practicing traditional midwife in the Detroit area. She is the only black traditional midwife in the area, possibly the state. I interviewed her in a variety of places, usually catching up with her as she ran between appointments or waiting for her son to finish a school program. I most enjoyed meeting her in her home, where photos of her patients and their families surrounded her. She remains in contact with most of "her" families. These families are mostly African American, sometimes from Africa or of Arabic descent. (The Detroit area has one of the highest populations of Arabic peoples in the United States.) She is selective of her clientele, carefully screening out any potentially risky births. She has not found that any of the patients were motivated to contact her because of an absence of health care coverage. In addition, because of the intensity and rigor of the birthing processes, Mama Leslie requires that the pregnant woman have some other familial or community support. She interviews the pregnant woman and her family extensively before entering a partnership with them. Her payment is a flat rate for the entire process, including pre- and postpartum visits. However, the payment is based on a sliding scale, taking the circumstances of the families into account. She limits the number of patients with whom she will work because of the time required for each patient. Now she limits the distance, but she will travel as well. She told of working with a pregnant woman who was over an hour's distance away. Because of extreme circumstances, she had to talk the panicked woman and her family through the birth by phone.

Midwifery has, for the most part, been taken into nursing programs, but there remain a few women who choose not to practice with direct connections to hospitals and medical doctors. Mama Leslie's alternative choice of medical practice is a calling. She is forty-two years of age, a single mother, and has been practicing for ten years. She continues to learn during conferences with other traditional midwives. She went into training and became a midwife during the time she was pregnant. Her pregnancy became her own conversion-to-midwifery story. Trying to find a gynecologist, she was dissatisfied with doctors who insisted on hospitalization, especially those intimating that caesarean birth was imminent. Hospitals and birth are antithetical concepts as far as Mama Leslie is concerned. Reflecting the troubled history of black Americans and white-owned and -operated hospitals, she stated with conviction: "Basically people die in hospitals." Her journey to becoming a midwife included coming to a new name on the African continent.

> I went to Africa and my spirit told me "If you're a midwife, and an African American midwife, in terms of life, you're Mama Leslie...." I know that in my lifetime, I'm going to reach a great amount of people, so what am I going to have to do to do that? And I want to empower my families to experience those things too. Who do I have to be to do that? I told God, "What did you put me in Detroit for, where I am Mama Leslie?"

Taking a holistic view, Mama Leslie understands the difficulties that occur during pregnancy as indicative of some other emotional or spiritual problem. Labor is an extended process, to be dealt with as it develops. She spoke of women in labor for five days. She refers to the medical profession's tendency to force delivery or perform a caesarean after so many hours of labor as "a technological birth, not a humanistic birth, not a holistic birth." From her perspective, babies who are being born have the power of choice over whether or not they want to come into the world; she believes that the birthing mothers are also able to control aspects of their bodies' operations, such as the amount of blood loss, barring hemorrhage.

Mama Leslie's objectives include healing families and breaking negative cycles. The sense of healing starts from her personal commitment to grow. "It's about conditionings and breaking those conditionings for me to be all I can be. Or to be in the world and not experience love, joy, and peace." The heart of her spirituality is simply stated: "There's only one truth, being one with God. Anything else is an illusion."

These three glimpses into the healing work of black midwives call forth a kind of wholesomeness of vision. These women resisted structures that limit them and found ways to work for and within their communities. Their roles had been more significant in the early to mid-twentieth century. But even today, the spirit of the grannies continues to urge us to share in that wholesome vision. A very few, like Mama Leslie, try to live that vision in a consumption-driven world.

There may be some important things we need to recapture from the grannies' sense of vocation: a desire to participate in our professional lives as a calling rather than a career; a new identification of the importance of the humanity of black folk; or learning to honor those that came before, in all the complexity of their responses to the American experiment. The respect for and recovery of the meanings, not necessarily the methods, of the black midwives is itself a healing process. Their relationships with God are instructive and also call all Christian Americans to reconsider the meaning of their faith and how they live it. In the grannies' stories, we also trace how black women's contributions to the American culture are so easily rendered unimportant. To recover these stories is another form of healing as well.

> Today the voices of granny midwives are largely silenced within their own communities. They have been labeled as ignorant and superstitious, as a problem or unhygienic. Yet when they were allowed to practice, they diligently carried out their duties and achieved excellent results.... The midwives who were interviewed for this study successfully delivered over four thousand babies. They were empowered and provided care that was both medically safe and heartfelt. This compels us to ask: what have we gained compared to what we have lost?[23]

Girl/Friends, Sister/Friends

The mere fact that you can be around some other black women and share what's going on in your life is a big help. And the other part is sisterhood, and my concept of sisterhood is a group of women being able to work together around a project. And there's a benefit in that.... See, when sisters are worried about how I'm gonna feed my kids, how I'm going

*to get to work, to pay my light bill, it's a little difficult to be
thinking about I got all this power. But I do think that power
comes from within the group — I know that's what helped me
evolve. I know that there's a group of powerful women out
here. I can pick up the phone and I can call. It doesn't mean
they got any money, but when we come together, it's almost
like we got something spiritual, something magical about that.
It's also made me kind of fearless.*
— AZANA, interviewed in Detroit, 1997

The connections among black people are certainly survival-based
skills, born of a shared history and current experiences of race and
class oppressions. This is a form of shared communication, but it
is not automatic or genetic. At one time, black people called this
"soul," but since the term has been co-opted by the media, the
meaning has been lost as "soul" is applied to everything. One of my
respondents tried to define the connections among black people.

There are connecting points. And it depends on so much. It
seems like the points come when there are folks who are connected with their own spirituality and their own uniqueness
and their own power. Their own sense of who they are, their
sense of their own personhood, their own lack of feeling threat-
ened by other people. Their own sense of "there's enough...."
[Their] lack of fear. [And then connections happen] sometimes
just by sight. I was in Ireland and just seeing another person
of African descent....Just a smile. (Frances, interviewed in
Detroit, 1996)

Frances used the term "community" and talked so often of the spirit
during our conversation that I finally asked her, "What is spirit?"
She responded: "One of the things I thought about was feeling spirit,
the various places I felt the spirit. One was the Baby Grand [a local
nightclub] when Jimmy Smits was playing. It was awesome. All
these people in all this space and there was a spirit there." Black
women's sense of girlfriends or sister/friends is related to this spirit.

The movie *Waiting to Exhale*, based on the novel by Terry McMillan, became a popularized sign of positive self-images for many black women: here were some sisters who mostly had good jobs, dressed well, and took charge of their lives. But black feminist author bell hooks took exception to this common idea:

> Lots of us went to see *Waiting to Exhale* expecting to enjoy a film about four black women friends coping with life and relationships, yet could not relate to the shallow, adolescent nonsense we saw on the screen. . . . What I saw was not women talking about love or the meaning of marriage or partnership, but women being obsessive about men, material success and petty competition with other women, especially white women. No doubt it helps crossover appeal to set up a stereotypically racist and sexist conflict between white women and black women competing to see who will win the man in the end. . . . Nothing has been more depressing than to hear some black women saying this film is a "realistic portrayal" of their experience.[24]

hooks's critique gets to the heart of the problems of many of the black women/girlfriends in plays, movies, and television programs that are popular today. Too much of the media-produced image centers on go-shopping-have-lunch friendships that might be set in workplaces or college campuses or neighborhoods but basically give the message that black women are "just" women, doing the same things as other women.

It is a major contention of this book that those "we're all alike" days have not arrived. Because African American women do face challenges in surviving workplaces and schools and families, sister/friends become powerful allies. Like granny midwives, the women who serve as support systems for other black women provide an invaluable network. As one black woman wrote:

> For who but a sister can you call up at 2:00 a.m. in the middle of the week and ask, "Do you have time to talk?" Who but a sister can you go to on payday to borrow twenty dollars to tide

you over? Who but a sister...can you gossip and laugh with, tears rolling down your cheeks, asses sliding off the chairs, bodies rolling on the floor in spasms?[25]

These words seem to highlight the popular portrayals of black women as friends, the late night call and the laughter. But the author clarified the *why* of black women learning to nurture each other. She stated:

We [black women] use each other's strength and tenacity to fight the stress that would put us in our graves before our time.... Stress does not heal; it infects; it's only satisfied when you're dead. It is the venom that gets into all black women's blood, causing our bodies to swell and explode, extinguishing our lives. But we have learned to create balm-yards to mix potions and perform a laying on of hands, to share our magic so that we can vanquish the stress that slaps us in the face every day.[26]

The humor and sassiness that black women can bring to the conversations about dealing with stress, especially the stresses that come from coping with incidents of racism, sexism, and classism, are important coping methods. It is healthy to put these stressors into perspective or learn other strategies for dealing with them. However, as one of my respondents pointed out, it is important for black women to separate from competitiveness during these conversations, because a sister will say something in honesty that the listener may not want to hear. This type of relationship takes maturity, and not every woman will want to be part of it; the "Exhale" party may be easier for some than listening to hard truths.

Learning to disclose personal truths and, conversely, listening to others' pain are important aspects of creating "balm-yards" among sister/friends.

To truly listen is to give attention, significance, and verification to the reality of women's anguish. It is to develop a counter cultural valuation that is especially needed in a world of denial. In our society, dispassionate detachment is valorized as the most "professional" stance for engaging the problems of others. And because the social construction of black women's worth too often rests upon the assertion of their indomitable, unceasing strength, the need for empathetic, affirming listening can appear even less obvious.[27]

One national organization has worked to improve the health of African American women. The National Black Women's Health Project (NBWHP) uses the power of sisters listening to each other as the primary method to achieve their ends. The organization has other objectives, but I focus here on the importance of their work in sister-ing, emphasizing one local chapter.

Begun in the 1980s, the NBWHP has been and continues to be concerned with comprehensive health care issues for African American women. In an effort to contribute to national health policy, the national office moved from Atlanta to Washington, D.C., in 1996. The result of this move created distancing from African American women's everyday lives. The work of the NBWHP can remain significant to black women's daily lives only through the efforts of the local chapters.

I attended meetings and interviewed members of the local chapter of Detroit Metropolitan Black Women's Health Project. The DMBWHP declares that it is

> committed to defining, promoting, and maintaining the physical, mental, spiritual, economic and emotional well-being of Black women. Therefore our mission is to facilitate the empowerment and wellness of women of African descent, their families, and future generations and communities globally. For us, health is not merely the absence of illness, but the active promotion of wellness. (Mission Statement, Detroit Metropolitan Black Women's Health Project)

Like the national organization, the DMBWHP focuses on black women's well-being, but they address the issues in meetings and self-help groups. The absence of self-care was often reported by members in interviews and within meetings. The interviews supported the concept that a poor health environment promotes life-threatening illnesses such as cancer and heart disease. The major stresses of being black and women repeatedly highlighted the draining daily demands that the women were forced to meet.

The meetings were integral to the life of the local organization, another form of sister-ing. Each meeting began with a "check-in." Standing in a circle, members and attendees shared information about themselves: "Name one positive thing that happened to you this week." "What health challenge are you facing now?" They called for "Disclosure, not exposure"; this philosophy is also the basis for their self-help groups.

Melody is a member who pointed out that the DMBWHP is the only African American group to which she belongs that has a diverse membership of African American women. She stated: "Every other group I belong to is for only a certain class or color, though we don't talk about that. [At DMBWHP meetings] you meet as equals and discuss the things going on in your life. It's not about how much this sister is making or anything else" (Melody, interviewed in Detroit, 1996).

Lisa discussed the personal impact of DMBWHP. The other members served as a community that gave her emotional and spiritual support to leave an unfulfilling job and write for a living. Lisa discussed her experiences: "For many of us, like myself, it was the first time I had been around all black women [and found out] what magic is." The experience caused her to weep. "I didn't know I had that many tears in me. I was so used to being responsible. Each of us with our own pocketful of healing came together and saved each other's lives" (Lisa, interviewed in Detroit, 1996).

There are several relevant points about how these meetings functioned in the participants' lives. The participants were called to focus on themselves and their own survival as black women, becoming self-aware. As a result, the women's own lives and experiences were immediately validated as worthy topics of discussion and reflection. As Melody stated, there was a conscious effort to build community, across lines of economics, religion, or sexual preference. When these efforts are successful, connections are made. In the work of the Project, healing becomes an underlying theme: the efforts to promote healing of social divisions and the wellness of the women participants serve as hallmarks of their work.

The self-help groups are conducted outside of the meeting times. These are set up as small groups of women, no more than ten, who meet in homes or wherever the most privacy can be achieved. The self-help groups are not homemade medical sessions, but challenge the participants to genuinely focus on themselves, to talk about not their children or mothers or jobs, but what they feel and experience and what that may be doing to their souls, bodies, or minds. One writer described the experience:

> Each person listens intently as another talks about her life predicament, to which everyone seems able to relate. Heads nod, murmured "uh-huhs" punctuate the testimony, and there's so much hugging. One hears over and over: "Sister, I know just how you feel!" At the end, members thank one another for sharing intimate details of their lives.[28]

The leaders of the self-help groups receive training to keep the sessions on focus. They are particularly trained to note and challenge the tendencies of many black women to avoid intense self-focus.

Frances, who is considered by the chapter as the guru of self-help groups, explained that

> the key elements . . . are safety, security, and opportunity. Demonstrate that we can create community anywhere. Women often say, "This is the first time I've been able to talk about myself and have someone really listen." A woman gets to focus on herself, to experience acceptance by a number of folks and to increase her own self-esteem and power. (Frances, interviewed in Detroit, 1996)

Sister/friends, like granny midwives, can give African American women opportunities to find new ways to give birth. Giving birth is not just a biological issue, but includes self-discovery and growth. Novelist Charlotte Watson Sherman phrased these connections eloquently.

> How can we not love the image of ourselves reflected in the beauty and strength of another Black woman? When the forces of racism and sexism and classism and homophobia align themselves against our spirits, it is often to another Black woman that we turn for comfort and reassurance that we are OK. The love and wisdom of our Black women friends revitalizes us as we support each other so that no more of us need fall from the weight of fighting oppression as we live our lives. Despite differences in class, skin color, hairstyle, educational background, sexual orientation, and other things that can divide us, Black women will continue to provide sanctuary for each other. What would we do without our sisterfriends?[29]

The next chapter begins an investigation of issues dealing with African American women and sexuality. The complex issues of sexuality assist in understanding black women's relationships, healings, and embodied spirituality.

FOUR

HEALING IN LOVE

I don't think we know what our sexuality is. The word "acculturation" is not strong enough. We're seeking assimilation [because] "it'll give me power." It is about an image — power, prestige, privilege and wealth — and those are white men's things. — DONZETTA, interviewed in Detroit, 2003

This chapter discusses black women's sexuality as a locale in need of healing. The chapter cannot cover all things about black women's sexuality; that topic would require several books. Instead, chapter 4 describes some sets of relationships that lead to the brokenness that African American women can experience through the very human expressions of sexuality. Many of the topics in the chapter contain language that African Americans are taught not to say.

Rather than a place for tapping power, sexuality often becomes spiritually, mentally, and physically draining: how to live up to gendered social expectations while others determine the best "you." The basic denial of self by black women has many similarities to the pressures on women in other cultures. The similarities also become a basis for conversation and coalition building, as indicated by the November 2003 "SisterSong Women of Color Reproductive Health and Sexual Rights Conference" held at Spelman College in Atlanta.

But there are some distinctions that need expression for African American women where race gets tied into the gender role equation in crippling ways. Maintaining an image — with hair and clothes presenting a socially determined self — is linked with being "good" black women who will attract "good" black men. When class issues are inevitably added, African American women too often become sources of comedy: the Whoopi Goldberg character in the 1990s movie *Ghost* brought howls of laughter when she got "dressed up" for a business meeting. African American women are pressured socially to accept and live up to an approved image of womanhood — and the consequences for establishing love relationships are profound. One woman baldly stated, "Who wants to be alone?" Another woman paraphrased a commercial to tell another story: "African American women are the loneliest people on the planet."

The pressures to conform are not mere processes of socialization but basic denials of self. The problem related to spirituality or religious life is in recognition of what it means for a person to pray or to know the Divine. What kind of God made African American women so flawed and so imperfect that they cannot be loved? What attributes does this God have who created black women as cosmic jokes? How can African American women claim we are created in God's image if we are constantly dishonest about our "selves"? These forms of repression and denial can represent social and personal crises that flow into the religious life, creating its own level of stress. That a healthy spirituality does not flourish under constant stress contrasts with the masculinized view that states that crisis smashes through our complacency to make us humble before God.[1] Quite often, women, especially African American women, do not need to be reminded to be humble like "servants." As womanist theologian Jacquelyn Grant discussed, perhaps we need to learn the importance of being disciples instead of promoting the sanctity of servanthood.[2]

All of these issues are woven into the many layers of the need for black women and men in the United States to recover from the oppressions of damaged sexuality. Chapter 4 focuses on this need from several angles. The ways that African American women's bodies are colonized (reconnecting to a theme from chapter 1), policed through gender, thereby constructing a black woman's sexuality, are addressed in this chapter. The second part of the chapter explores sexism in African American communities. Sexism creates the crisis of heterosexism in black communities and is explored in the

third section, along with issues around marriage. The final section
on black lesbians brings to the surface a variety of other issues that
are related to the push for heterosexist utopia. The issues raised by
these relationships are not free-standing but transition to chapter 5
for further analysis.

Viewing Black Women as Colonized

The idea of black bodies as colonized may seem inappropriate: after
all, a body is not a land. Yet, scholars are coming to recognize that
the ways people of color are treated *are* forms of colonization. The
first chapter specifically looked at how these colonizing effects were
part of the period of legal enslavement. Today, there are still systems in place — such as publicly negative views of black women
as mothers — that enforce control of black women's bodies. These
are real power relations, between black people and the majority culture, not political terminology or philosophical rhetoric. Black lives
are on the line within the systems in which they live, yet the attitude is often held by other people in the United States that African
Americans should just stop crying "victim" to take advantage of
the tremendous economic and educational benefits that are available to anyone who works hard. *Real* poverty, I have heard several
academics and ministers state, is to be found in the "Third World"
countries that are underdeveloped. African Americans do not know
what *real* poverty is like, these experts claim, and nobody hears
those "Third-Worlders" complaining.

The poverty-comparison-and-dismissal view silences the voices
of black people in the United States as well as the people in
other countries as their relative states of being are analyzed according to the measuring sticks of the dominant group. Further,
this kind of analysis constructs antagonistic relationships between
the oppressed groups that are victimized by the same imperialistic colonizers, continuing to divide and conquer. There are better
ways to think about who populates the "third world." Anthropologist Kristin Koptiuch used the phrase "third worlding at home" as
a way to discuss these power relations. "Forms of power/knowledge

generally associated with the colonial and postcolonial exploitation of a distant third world are also becoming increasingly apparent in the treatment of U.S. minorities."[3] In other words, being "Third World-ed" at home signals inequitable, embedded power relationships of definable groups with the dominant culture and within a global framework. These power relationships construct the "Other" who falls outside the power grid. These constructions become so accepted as to be rendered invisible and "natural." The processes of constructions can be recognized in the ways that black women's bodies continue to be colonized. Awareness of how Americans in general tend to think about black women's bodies/sexuality is an important first step in analyzing their meanings.

African American women are not viewed as desirable life partners or romantic figures by the general U.S. public. Thinking of African American women as desirable, redeemable (no matter the crime or flaw), or socially acceptable and competent seldom happens. African American women are more likely to have their sexuality viewed as a sign of pathological or pitiful relationships. The portrayal of black women as sexual beings (or not) is easily captured through the imagery of the media. Several examples follow.

Some tout the presence of black women in movies and television, yet what has changed? The 1990s movie *The Bodyguard* presented Whitney Houston as a rich and successful singer who seduced one of her employees. A television program ten years later, *The Parkers*, depicts a black mother and daughter who desperately seek men, with the mother going so far as to lie in order to trick a man into marriage. In the 2004 Superbowl televised half-time program, the singer Janet Jackson showed a bare breast. Yet the young white man who ripped her clothing off was barely criticized while Jackson was blamed and censured. Are there any positive images? Perhaps the black female character that appeared in the last year of the television program *Friends* is significant; yet that role was so deracialized as to apologize for her race. African American women's sexual stereotypes are in place and American public perceptions are barely altered: teen mothers, women-headed households, and "crack" babies seem to capture the headlines and the public imagination — and implied pathologies of African American communities, women and men, continue. But the presentations of the incorrect or immoral lives of African Americans are not only in the media. More insidious presentations happen in other public places, such as among researchers. When negative research on African American women and men becomes the basis for government or business decisions, inequities are built into institutions, as the following longer example demonstrates.

A report that was distributed by the U.S. Census Bureau, "Racial-Ethnic and Gender Differences in Returns to Cohabitation and Marriage," was written by Philip Cohen and presented at the 1999 Annual Meeting of the Population Association of America. The Census version states as a preface, "This report is released to inform interested parties of research and to encourage discussions."[4] The initial questions to be asked are: who are the interested parties? With whom are these discussions to be held? The material that Cohen presents makes these questions important because he is discussing marriage and cohabitation premiums, concluding his study with questions about black women. Marriage "premiums" refer to the higher wages accorded those in certain living situations, that is, married. The premium is offered by the employer with the assumption that those in a household, presumably with children, need more income for reasonable support. The employee is considered less of a risk and more stable if married, compared with single people. Marriage premiums were more likely to go to men, with the presumption that they were most likely the heads of the household. The attendant assumption is that women employees have males on whom to rely for income; therefore, the women need less income. Additionally, women were viewed as less stable in the workforce because of possible pregnancy and child-rearing responsibilities. While premiums of this sort are supposedly illegal under equal opportunity laws — and although feminists have battled this thinking, hoping for parity in the workplace — Cohen's report indicates that equality is a long way off. His inclusion of a "cohabitation" premium only indicates a new category in the workplace — not that inequities have been reduced. Underlying Cohen's research, as will be seen, is a condemnation of cohabitation with an expectation of the normality of heterosexual males earning more than females and therefore the correctness of marriage premiums.

Cohen used Census data and secondary sources from select literature. He compared the rates of marriage premiums and smaller cohabitation premiums given to white, African American, and Hispanic men in some workplace settings over a span of years and suggested that higher productivity is at least tangentially related to marriage. Women had different rates of this so-called premium, and Cohen found "Black women have the largest cohabitation premium, more than three times the premium for white women... and substantially larger than the premium for all three groups of men."[5] His conclusion sends out warning signals:

> The fact that black men and women both have marriage and cohabitation premiums has implications for inequality among black workers, especially given lower black marriage rates. The apparent mutual selection of higher-earning black men and women would contribute to increases in family-level income inequality. That is, at the same time marriage rates are low, those with higher wages are more likely to be married or cohabitating together. *The high cohabitation premium for black women also might suggest that black couples are less likely to marry when women are earning more, creating a hurdle between the formation of cohabiting unions and marriage. That is, black women's earnings might be more of an obstacle to marriage than they are to forming a cohabiting union.*[6]

Cohen's argument assumes a certain kind of marriage and definition of success as imperative to American life. Normality, as he knows it, lays a sledgehammer to black social relations. Cohen makes no attempt to interview or interact with the blacks, Hispanics, or whites for whom he constructs reality: he sticks with paper trails that support his own cultural perspective. His conclusion implies a world of inequality with causal factors of cohabitation premiums for African Americans, helping them to avoid marriage, and higher wages for black women. The preface, encouraging discussion, leads to wondering what kind of discussions would take place about the income or marital status of African Americans, especially women. Other questions are born of the first. Why is it necessary to compare cohabitation with marriage rates in the first place? Where is the discussion of the legal ramifications of a marriage or cohabitation premium? To whom is this comparison a matter of concern? And, most importantly, why publish this particular information under the auspices of the U.S. Census?

With slick language, Cohen's 1999 report accuses African American women's earnings of destroying families. Cohen's work aligns itself with the 1965 Moynihan Report. Following references to the impact of "personal prejudice" because of the "racist virus in the American bloodstream" and the "centuries of sometimes unimaginable mistreatment," the 1965 report found that the real problem to black social and economic advancement is the "family structure."

> The evidence — not final, but powerfully persuasive — is that the Negro family in the urban ghettos is crumbling. A middle-class group has managed to save itself, but for vast numbers of the unskilled poorly educated city working class the fabric of conventional social relationships has all but disintegrated.... [7]

African Americans' social relationships are continually pathologized, with black women consistently carrying the blame for the disease. Throughout the American landscape, black women are implicitly blamed for deviant sexuality of cohabitating and single parenting that destroys family and "the fabric of conventional social relationships." These patterns of blaming black women, of demonizing our sexualities, of ridiculing attempts to make or improve our families, of analyzing us from an arrogant distance, of subjecting us to constant surveillance and critique, of using a comparison base of a white middle-class "standard": these are all processes of "third-worlding."

African American women are judged for our sexualities when sexuality, like prayer, is personal, reflecting patterns of socialization. Yet, in a country that claims the legal protection of the privacy of its citizens, African American women's bedrooms have been under close and constant scrutiny. For African American women, both black and white communities (at minimum) contour their sexualities as a matter of public concern. Sexuality, like prayer, has become politicized by those who are white, male, and affluent. These are processes of colonizing African American women's bodies.

Practices of connecting race and sex developed along with the colonization of the United States. The practices are seen in the recounting of one historian of the development of legislation in the colony of Virginia.

> The success of laws punishing race mixing seems clear. Hostility to interracial marriage and children of mixed ancestry grew during the eighteenth century.... By the time of the Revolution, Virginia effectively regulated interracial sex. Most whites accepted the norms, created in the seventeenth century, that they should never marry a black. White men understood that they could have relations with their slave without suffering any penalty.... Most white women, on the other hand, understood the severity of penalties for a relationship with a black man.[8]

Virginia was not isolated in such legislation. The control of sexual behavior became a matter of policy. Ann Stoler details this practice across international lines:

> Gender-specific sexual sanctions demarcated positions of power by refashioning middle-class conventions of respectability, which, in turn, prescribed the personal and public boundaries of race.... Ultimately inclusion or exclusion required regulating the sexual, conjugal and domestic life of *both* Europeans in the colonies and their colonized subjects.[9]

This brief look at history uncovers important facts in understanding the continued colonization of African American women's bodies. The colonizing process had a distinct purpose in controlling the populations and has become embedded in American society. The process credits black women with powers they simply do not

have: to destroy black families or emasculate black men or prevent economic growth in black communities. The racialized texts
of these beliefs about black women's sexualities continue, in some
form, both inside and outside black communities. These texts have
become so embedded that black women expend enormous energy
and time trying to counter, ignore, or live them. This process results
in a devastating denial of our selves. Carolyn Martin Shaw, a black
feminist anthropologist, wrote: "My sense of myself as a woman
was not constructed only through mass media. But if I were looking in my community for women who thought of themselves as
good women and as sexual, then my talk was once again well nigh
impossible."[10]

Sexism in Black Communities

At the end of July 2003, I was walking with friends in downtown
Brooklyn when we passed a group of black men from the Israelite
Church of God and Jesus Christ, speaking from soapboxes. They
were dressed in an assortment of Eastern-looking clothing, hel-
meted and in black velvet uniforms of some kind. They spoke
over microphones to the mostly black audience, conveying messages about their religion, actively proselytizing the passing crowds.
One of their loudest, most virulent messages was about the errors
of black women who did not know how to be women who should
be silent in society. In fact, the speakers claimed, the Bible clearly
delineates the roles of women: as submissive to men. African American women have totally separated themselves from God with their
improper disrespect of black men. One of the members of my party
turned to us and said, "I never thought I'd hear misogyny preached
on a street corner."

But any street corner, living room, or pulpit may find some black
group advocating race-based sexism. The race-based sexism is not
limited to marriage relationships. African American community
members often expect the men to "take care" of the women. This
taking-care does not always translate into the same kind of pa-
triarchy, with full power, money, and control that white men can

more readily access. Instead, many African American women decry the lack of men, and some very financially independent black women complain that they are tired of "taking the man's role." Black feminist bell hooks stated:

> Contrary to popular belief, black folks have always upheld the primacy of patriarchy if only symbolically. Whether males have been present in black families in the United States or not, many black females in their roles as heads of households assumed an authoritarian, symbolically patriarchal stance. ... Most black women validated the superiority of maleness, the importance of the male role even as they may also have critiqued black men for not assuming that role.[11]

The term "patrifocal" may well describe African American familial relationships. This is the reason that "mothers love sons but raise daughters" and that families often expect that the males be accorded special privileges. This is the reason that independent black women brag that "I'll let him *think* he's in charge" rather than entering into honest relationships. "But he's a man" still excuses many sexual excesses and violent actions in black communities. Women across distinctive cultures and nations have these experiences. Yet for African American women, the issue of racism is ever-present: we women should do anything that seems to be demanded of us in personal relationships to "save" the race. Womanist ethicist Traci West recorded the words of one black woman: "There's this dictum, I would say in the black community, that men come first, that black men come first, black men are the ones that are oppressed.... Everyone else is a kind of fodder for their tribulations. That's what it means to be a black woman."[12] Social judgment against the noncompliant woman, by the rest of the black community, is harsh. The purported inability of black women to "support" black men or to be "real" women becomes the theme in blaming African American women for black men "turning" to the womanly arms of white women.

In these thought patterns, connections to racism are blatantly present because black families never had the opportunities or the access to wealth that has maintained white families — and white women — across generations into their present comfortable niches. This may be one of the most pressing reasons for black women to avoid any involvement with movements for women's justice that use the name "feminist." Most white women have taken for granted the privileges they have received, and their political interests are often woven into fabrics of some feminist movements. The history of feminist movements tells unfortunate stories of African American women's exclusion or alienation. The aims of many white feminists still do not address African American women's concerns or, in the twenty-first century, presume that the needs of both groups are the same. Sometimes the "liberation" that black women seek is to have the privileges of white women that they have been denied. To many African American women, the lives of many white women look like luxury in the face of their own. It is difficult to align with a cause where lunch meetings are held in clubs that you cannot afford.

Yet there are black women who bring liberation home to African American communities. Womanist theologian Delores Williams is one. She wrote of distinctions between the goals of black and white American women:

> White feminists struggle for women's liberation *from male domination* with regard for such *priority* issues as rape, domestic violence, women's work, female bonding, inclusive language, the gender of God, economic autonomy for women, and heterosexism. Black women liberators would perhaps consider *women's liberation and family liberation from white-male-white-female domination* with regard for such priority issues as physical survival and spiritual salvation of the family (with equality between males and females); the re-distribution of goods and services in the society (so that white families no longer get the lion's share of the economic, educational, political, and vocational resources available in every social class); encountering God as family (masculine and feminine, father, mother, and child); ending white supremacy, male supremacy

(or any gender supremacy), and upper-class supremacy in all American institutions.[13]

Her words powerfully set out the realities of black women's gendered life: it is problems not merely with men, but with the embedded inequities in American social structures that creates havoc in perceptions of our colonized sexualities. Enacting sexuality through sex partners and acts, in this framework, serves as a border separating the colonized/natives (black) from the colonizers/rulers (white). Therefore, acts of sex become borders that need policing and thereby maintain the privileged status of white Americans. When African Americans accept these ideas as normal and begin patrolling the borders, the initial motivation may be protecting black communities from cruelty, but the end result is that whiteness is secured in its position of dominance.

Sexism in black communities also damages African American psyches: what does it mean to be a whole human being in this world? Black feminist anthropologist Cheryl Rodriguez stated: "I realize that while growing up, I witnessed Black women enduring many forms of oppression within the Black community. Sexist beliefs and practices were as common as rain and often appeared to be the natural order of life."[14]

Sexism is not something that churches in black communities have addressed. Black churches too often encourage small visions of black women's lives. Women members might cater to the pastor and other males of the congregation, reinforcing ideas of girls' and women's lesser importance in black communities. Womanist sociologist Cheryl Townsend Gilkes stressed another dimension of churches' reinforcement of negative gender structuring, one that builds upon images of beauty and what has been called African Americans' color complex.

> Ironically, black churches are often pastored by men who are most fiercely committed to the dominant culture's notions of beauty and do not see these notions as white, male, and exclusionary. Those notions are affirmed and reaffirmed from the pulpit to the door, often in quite subtle ways. The prettiest and

lightest little girls in the church are often encouraged in ways that allow them to discover that their visual status is a resource for success; they are socialized to be "cute" and to grow up to be beautiful. In contrast, the darker and plumper girls are encouraged to be serious, develop leadership skills, and above all, do well in school. Some black women have called this the "pretty-ugly" syndrome in black culture.[15]

Both inside and outside churches, the constructions of African American women's sexuality are played against those of black men. The belief that men must "control" women becomes a central theme. The fear that too-strong black women destroy the manhood of black men is especially intense in love relationships. William Oliver is a criminologist who explained black male/female domestic violence in this way:

> In most incidents involving the male versus female dyad, black males will respond with violence toward females who they perceive as trying to control them, make them look bad in the eyes of others or manipulate them. Hence, when black males engage in violence against black females, it is because they have defined the situation as one in which the female's actions constitute a threat to their manhood . . . issues related to the maintenance of the tough-*guy* image are predominate with respect to the intrapersonal decision to use violence.[16]

The relationships between black men and women do not seem to improve among African American young adults. At several predominantly white college campuses I visited, from Washington, D.C., to Texas, black women students have reported to me that black men will not date them, but rather select white, Hispanic, or Asian women. African American men students will be friendly or study with, but not actually date, the black women students. I usually get a response of resigned laughter when I ask African American women students why they do not choose to date outside the boundaries of race. One young woman, however, told me with embarrassment that she had been "talking seriously" with a white male student.

Bakari Kitwana is a political scientist with expertise in the music business. He analyzes the age group of African Americans born between 1964 and 1985, which he terms the "hip-hop generation." In matters of love relationships, Kitwana reflects that young black men of the hip-hop generation are the first to grow up with feminism and women's rights as a part of their lives. Yet, the lyrics of rap music and the accompanying videos generally reflect negative views of black women, regularly referred to as "bitches." The label has been controversial among black women of that age group: is "bitch" really a negative word for black women or just generational slang?

Further, the relationships between young African American men and women are being shaped by beliefs held by many African American men. Kitwana cites the rape trials and convictions of rapper Tupac Shakur and boxer Mike Tyson as important events in defining hip-hop generation male understandings of black women. Four of the points he raised are: "Black male group loyalty is central to young Black male identity.... Many hip hop generation men lack interest in or understanding of feminism.... The objectification of women has intensified in our lifetime.... The intense focus on materialism in our generation is undermining many relationships."[17]

These ideas emphasize that the desires of black women for the financial benefits and respect accorded to white women and the desire of black communities for men to be protectors has shifted from those of the nineteenth and early twentieth centuries to those described above. Today, the ideas of being a woman or a man are romanticized in many African American communities: the romanticism is really about being assimilated into white society. Being a "real" man or woman gets twisted up with proving commitment to American ideals. Thus, the authenticity of a racialized identity is fused to a black, authentic, gendered identity.

Womanist theologian Kelly Brown Douglas has begun a discussion of the problems and complexities of sexism in black communities. Her work is groundbreaking, bringing these discussions into the dimensions of black church life. Simply put, how can the black Christian community continue to implicitly or explicitly uphold sexism? The answers to that question are not simple. Douglas grounds the reasons for these problems in the deep and dividing legacy of white sexual assault on black people, a form of colonization. She states: "A history of having their sexuality exploited and used as a weapon to support their oppression has discouraged the Black community from freely engaging sexual concerns."[18]

Loving Men

Issues of relationships between black women and men carry the sexist baggage discussed in the section above. Black individuals and couples work through and around these problems, to become healthy in love relationships. But they are often the exceptions because of the socially constructed drive behind sexism, through the pressures of heterosexism. Heterosexism is, basically, the establishment of total vision of the absolute normality of heterosexual relationships with the corresponding total deviance of anything that is not. Women's and men's behaviors are held up to often shifting, ambiguous heterosexist measures that are socially determined, and demand certain ways of behaving or appearing. These behaviors shift over time instead of being tied to biology: what "good" women did in 1904 will not be the same thing that is expected in 2004. However, heterosexism presents acceptable behaviors as having "always been this way." This establishes the normalizing feature of heterosexism: we have a difficult time seeing or even questioning those behaviors deemed acceptable because they are norms. Aren't they? Black women's and men's lives are informed by heterosexism, as is most of American society.

However, for black women and men, heterosexism has become a measure of being an "authentic" African American. In part, the social pressure to conform begins outside the black community, with the judgments of, for example, the Moynihan or Cohen reports as guidelines, to which black people respond defensively. The pressure of being under the surveillance and critiques of white Americans adds to the pressures of proving that we are "better" in our families, in our love relations, in our being men or women. Conversely, the conversations among groups of black women often denigrate how this white woman or that white man acted in a perverse manner. In fact, black women and men often set up alternate critiques of white Americans that "blame" them for African American homosexuality, incest, and child sexual molestation while black families' woes are dismissed as the continued effects of enslavement by white people. Being a "righteous" brother or sister sets up heterosexism with the weight of choosing sides, really black or only a white pretender.

The maintenance of the correct image gets tied to appearance, and black people judge each other by looks, a fully American pastime. The pressures to conform to a certain style of dress are tremendous, and self-esteem is tied to clothing. All of these issues of bodily conforming train African Americans to respond to surveillance.

Attendance at church is one of the major dress-up events for many African Americans; a mother complained to me of spending two hundred dollars for an Easter outfit that her daughter would only wear that day. This kind of complaint is not unusual: I have spoken with African American women of limited financial means who complain about the costs of maintaining these images, but continue to participate in being "dress poor." Getting hair and nails professionally done becomes part of a dress code for young black women. The hairstyle that is usually expected in the Detroit area is straightened, with a resistance to natural hair. The pressure to conform to hairstyling norms begins in elementary schools. One woman whose husband and children have natural hair reported to me that her daughter, entering the sixth grade, was told by African American school officials to change her hair or she would never get a job; the child's acceptability was tied to the straightness of her hair. The judgment of the femininity of black women is tied to appearance: what man wants a woman who is not feminine?

In a similar way, an African American woman is socially pressured to prove her femininity by being in a relationship with a black man, reinforcing the heterosexist images. For black women, the pressure to "get" a man heightens during the teenage years. This "getting" is tied to race loyalty. Yet, African American women's desperation indirectly denigrates men's dignity because, as the saying goes, "*Any* pair of pants will do." For many black women, especially those growing older, African American men's death and incarceration rates create greater panic to get and hold a man. These pressures do not happen in a vacuum, and there are agents in black communities that support a heterosexist view. I briefly discuss only two of them: the black romance novel and black churches.

The black romance novel is a relatively recent phenomenon, with record numbers of publications and sales. Some of the novels weave lessons into the plots, such as how black women and men found love while in historical settings. Some with plots in contemporary settings are centered on work themes. Some authors deal with issues of race within the plot line, such as finding love with a lighter/darker person. The romance genre was, in many ways, a natural area of interest for black women. The upsurge in the sales of these novels is not surprising when considering the combination of the desire/pressure to be in a relationship with men, the shortage of African American men, and the high number of single black women. The books by and large do not mirror the lives of white women and are very specific to the contexts of black women's lives. However, there is a parallel in the ways that the successful romantic end is viewed as a happily-ever-after, Westernized heterosexual commitment, preferably marriage. These books, despite the reflections of African American women's lives, apply more pressure to achieve a marriage that is marked by a monogamous, committed, male/female relationship that will produce children and income.

African American marriages are deeply influenced by heterosexism to conform to certain gender roles and to match the well-promoted image of the nuclear family. In applying pressure, heterosexism has powerful allies in most black churches. As an example, T. D. Jakes's Texas-based ministry is one that has unfortunately had great influence in African American communities. One young woman in the Dallas area described attending Jakes's church as going to a meat market: the women were there to be picked up by men and the men expected that the women were there for that reason. Jakes has extended his reach and produced a book series that defines a form of black "femininity." In one of the books, Jakes provided advice on women's roles and relationships with men and God. In one section, he berates men for thinking that wives must be weak or limited and offers this dubious praise:

> A virtuous woman will never do her man harm. She is a wife. She is a treasure. The sister is awesome! She is the kind of woman whose support makes the difference. Weak? I don't think so! She is the combustion in an engine. She is the steam in an iron. She "does him good and not evil." She is a doer! This girl is no dreamer; she is no idle threat. She delivers like a pizza shop; she is at the door, on the mark, and prepared for the need. It is no wonder that she causes smiles to break out whenever she comes. She is passive, but aggressive. Not so passive that she is not able to take the initiative, yet she is not so aggressive that she leaves him no role to play. The lady is a doer and she does him good! Do him, girl. He needs you.[19]

Jakes dehumanizes black women, seeing them as things — a pizza shop or steam — that will take care of men's needs. Black women's work, in this view, is for the good of men. Their own needs become subsumed by the needs of men. Throughout this construction, Jakes weaves scriptural references that offer a kind of biblical abuse in defining black women. for instance, the description of the "virtuous woman" above reads like updated maxims from the book of Proverbs, thereby seeming to lend Jakes's words greater authority. Through his book goals are set that settle African American women back into caretaking-everybody roles: of course smiles break out wherever she goes.

Jakes has tapped into a definite need among African American women that has expanded his influence in frightening ways. He has produced other books; his wife has written one about women's roles. Jakes sponsors plays that travel to black urban centers to focus on love relationships being saved by God, and he runs conferences around the country that help women discover their godly talent for being good women. Not surprisingly, he is now writing romance novels. Other black ministers through the country have discovered the cost benefits of helping African American women be all that men want them to be. Jakes has served as a role model in this updated form of pimping.

In this conflicted reality, African Americans have their own struggles with marriage. With the pressures of heterosexism already in place, marriage receives the additional pressures from the observations of dominant society. Like the seemingly scientific reports of Moynihan in the 1960s and Cohen in the 1990s, black marriages become a topic of study. African Americans, especially women, must be doing something wrong, as the words of the following study seem to indicate. "It is thus not divorce but the failure to marry that has led to such a momentous change in black family patterns. The marriage rate for African Americans has plummeted in the past third of [the twentieth] century."[20] In this analytical approach by Stephan and Abigail Thernstrom, without surprise, African American women continue to receive blame for the falling marriage rate. The Thernstroms continue their analysis:

> Today a clear majority of African-American women aged fifteen to forty-five have never been married, as compared with just a third of their white counterparts.... Many fewer black women are marrying, and yet they continue to have children — which was not the case in an earlier era.... For much of the African-American population, marriage and childbearing have become almost completely dissociated.[21]

Unlike the Moynihan and Cohen studies, the Thernstroms read a nonexistent past of mostly married African American women without a historical framework, but strengthening their pattern of blaming women. Like the Moynihan and Cohen studies, the Thernstroms connect the numbers of married African Americans with any poor economic conditions of black communities; therefore, the lack of wealth in black communities is tied to black women. What is clearly wrong with these studies — in addition to the absence of the people being studied — is the lack of historical context: the economics of African American communities cannot be linked simplistically to marriage rates. Yet this theme has been played too well since Moynihan's 1960s script. The heterosexism and the sexism of this script are never mentioned. It is implied that: *if* black Americans stuck to white Americans' prescriptions of gender roles, *if* black men got jobs like white men, *if* black people had families that matched the white middle-class model, if black people did these things, then there would be no poverty in black communities. The combined effects of enslavement, legal and habitual segregation, unequal education, lower incomes, restricted housing, lynching, rape, political disenfranchisement, poor health care while living in communities that were the primary targets of redistricting, claim by governmental eminent domain, drug running, and alcohol sales are ignored: it must be those black people's unwillingness to marry that causes today's problems.

These assumptions do affect black women and men's relationships — and African American women in particular ways. A kind of self-defeating spiral begins for black women, driven by heterosexism: black women are often viewed, as one young woman stated, "as good enough to screw but not good enough to *be* with." Attitudes about the sexual availability of black American women are spread far, and it is not unusual to hear men from different African countries repeat such stereotypes. But black women are still caught between the contradictions of the push to get a man and the stereotype of sexual libertine.

Adding to this image are the high numbers of black women who give birth without marriage. Within black communities, language has developed among younger women that names a connection with the biological fathers, the baby's daddy. There is a corresponding name for the woman, the baby's mama. Relationships are built around recognizing the child's life. References to these relationships are made in rap music, but what other images do young people have? The unhappiness and uneven success of older generations stand with many young people. Young black men witness the problems that have occurred when legal measures are taken against "deadbeat dads," becoming one more opportunity for control of black men's incomes and lives. Young women are still caught in the trap of "getting" a man. Bakari Kitwana states one hip-hop generationer's perspective:

> Baby mommas and baby daddies are a category unique to our generation. This is not to say that having children out of wedlock is unique to our generation. What's unique is this generation's open acceptance of it as the norm. As hip-hop generationers have come of age, the stigma that in previous generations was attached to having children outside of marriage has almost disappeared. This is partly due to the increase in divorce rates, which began among baby boomers in the mid-1960s. Many hip-hop generationers witnessed the divorce of their parents and do not view marriage as a panacea.[22]

For some people, "baby's daddy/mama" is sign of the further deterioration of African American families and communities. One black woman became quite vocal in her objections during a discussion, charging that the lack of morality among young black people is disgusting and shameful. However, is it more shameful than people of older generations who married because of a pregnancy and then were unable to maintain that marriage? Blaming each other does not help. What is needed is more thorough analysis on two levels. First, more extensive study of the pervasive influence of heterosexism in black communities is needed, especially how this concept shapes black children's expectations. The other area is in exploring the realities of marriage — the concepts, the operations, the cultural references, the social constructions — within black communities. Discussing these two areas would require longer studies than can be accommodated in these pages.

Loving Women

Black lesbians present one of the most direct challenges to heterosexism in African American communities because they contradict the role limits placed on black women. They also confront the heterosexism that exists in black communities. But these confrontations are minor when compared with a deeper problem: homophobia. If heterosexism totalizes the correctness and normality of male-female relationships, homophobia produces a climate in black communities of the total fear of same-sex relationships. Like all phobias, homophobia is not rational. People who are in same-sex relationships have not ended the world, a heterosexual cannot "catch" same-sex preference, and discussing homosexuality does not cause anyone's hair to fall out. Instead, the phobia insists that same-sex relationships be wrapped in religiosity, hammered with scriptural verse, and condemned, to the total denial of biological and psychological facts. Homophobia exists throughout the United States, among all races and all classes. In African American communities, homophobia is also wrapped in racial terms.

On one hand, African American homophobia is tied to heterosexism: "authentic" black men and women prefer love relationships with only the opposite sex, with the underlying message, "We are different from those perverse white people." Yet this does not tell the whole story, for certainly there are and have been individuals in African American communities who are not interested in the opposite sex for love relationships. Some black gay men are recognized and given an uncomfortable place in the community: stereotypes of hairdressers, choir directors, and other artistic persons are shrugged off, but grudgingly accepted. African American people involved in illegal enterprises are often sexually distrusted as "bad" influences. Performers and artists are also under suspicion. People in these fields are seen as those for whom anything goes sexually, and are contrasted with the "good" — that is, sexually moral — African Americans in Christian churches. The worlds on the edge of the "good" black world provide some safe, if stereotypical, space for black lesbian, gay, and bisexual people.

These patterns of denial and division create warped and dishonest realities, as shown in one author's discussion of the black male homosexual underground.

Rejecting a gay culture they perceive as white and effemi-
nate, many black men have settled on a new identity, with
its own vocabulary and customs and its own name: Down
Low. There have always been men — black and white — who
have had secret sexual lives with men. But the creation of an
organized, underground subculture largely made up of black
men who otherwise live straight lives is a phenomenon of the
last decade.... Most date or marry women and engage sexually with men they meet only in anonymous settings like
bathhouses and parks or through the Internet. Many of these
men are young and from the inner city, where they live in
a hypermasculine "thug" culture.... Most DL men identify
themselves not as gay or bisexual but first and foremost as
black. To them, as to many blacks, that equates to being
inherently masculine.[23]

By living in a climate of denial and secrecy, African American
women and men experience astronomical rates of AIDS/HIV, which
is discussed in greater detail in the next chapter. But there are
no statistics to locate the damage to black sexuality created by
homophobia, which, as Kelly Brown Douglas states so clearly, is
a continuation of a history of white sexual assault.

Homophobia does not reflect merely a close-minded sexual
bigotry by Black men and women. This is a phobia and
prejudice nurtured in large part by a history of White sexual exploitation. The case supporting homophobia in the
Black community reveals homophobia almost as a misguided
strategy for protecting Black lives and the integrity of Black
sexuality, as a necessary position to safeguard Black life
and freedom. Homosexuality is seen as threatening Black
well-being.[24]

As homophobia is affected by race in African American communities, so is it gendered. Black lesbians create even more discomfort
among African Americans. The case of Sakia Gunn, a fifteen-year-
old black lesbian who was murdered in Newark, New Jersey, on

May 11, 2003, is evidence of this homophobic discomfort. Gunn and her friends were approached by men whom they turned down. After the young women turned the men down, they were attacked. One of the men, Richard McCullough, stabbed Sakia Gunn to death. The murder has galvanized the black lesbian communities around the country, and multiple conversations are taking place across the Internet about this death. One woman wrote: "I know what it is like to be young and gay and scared, and full of bravado, wondering, always wondering if someone will try to hurt me. More than 20 years later, I know what it is like to see my sisters, my daughters, walk the same streets I did, trying to find their way home."[25]

In an online magazine, Kelly Cogswell and Ana Simo compared the lack of public response about Sakia Gunn's murder with the 1998 murder of Matthew Shepard, a gay white man, in Wyoming. Shepard's murder brought these kinds of hate crimes to public view; Gunn, the writers charge, is being erased:

> The problem here is that while white racism contributes significantly to Gunn's erasure from the media, and the modest turnout at the protest, it doesn't do much to explain the apathy of Newark's black mayor, Sharpe James, and his powerful black Democratic machine. Only homophobia explains why James' post-funeral pledge to meet with Gunn's family and local gay activists ... is always sometimes for the future. Only homophobia explains why new antigay behavior at Gunn's school, the West Side High School, has passed without comment or indignation from Mayor James.... And where are the professionally outraged activists like Al Sharpton who always appears en masse to hold politicos accountable when young black people are cut down by hate and no one is doing anything? ... The reason why Sakia Gunn was killed, and why her murder has faded from the headlines, is that both whites and blacks wish young black queers would disappear. Until things change, they will, thanks to violence, and AIDS, and hate.[26]

The fear of lesbians in black communities is real and is expanded to control the behavior of African American women. Who would want to be called a lesbian? And so the phobia spirals and embeds itself even more firmly. Womanist scholar Renita J. Weems exposes this aspect of homophobia and the different responses that might buy into or resist the pressure to conform.

> In light of the mindless homophobia (exacerbated by the hysteria surrounding AIDS) that exists in the Black community, the accusation of being a lesbian is most often a ploy to castrate a woman, to silence her, to scare her into obedience, to undermine her effectiveness before her peers and clients, and to remind her of her place. In some instances, it has been effective. For I've seen friendships terminate; I've seen women denounce other women to win male affection; and I've seen women turn in their placard and withdraw from a movement for fear of being labeled a lesbian. But then I've also seen heterosexual women embracing lesbian women in sisterhood, with no regard for who was looking, and marching together down mean streets on behalf of bereaved mothers in South Africa. And I've seen lesbian women raising funds for local battered-women shelters and woman-ing the phones all night at rape crisis centers.[27]

Weems's words end this section on a tenuous note of hope and healing. The hope is found in African American women finding ways across the barriers that have been constructed to contain them. The next chapter explores other results of the constructions of black sexuality discussed in these pages.

FIVE

SEXUALITY, HAZARD, AND HOPE

Healing needs to go on. If a woman experiences something as extraordinary as rape or domestic violence, I think that kills part of her soul and part of her spirit and it's part of you. It's almost eight years and I haven't been able to bring that part back to life. I've been able to find life in other areas but there's a part of me that's still dead and I refuse to accept that that part of me is dead forever. . . . I've experienced healing, but when you experience that kind of betrayal, I don't know how, how you recover from that . . . to learn to live again and to love yourself.
— MELODY, interviewed in Detroit, 1996

Chapters 2 and 3 explored relationships of African American women as mothers, aunties, midwives, and sister/friends and had positive overtones. Yet, in matters of sexuality, the issues become murky, much less positive, and fraught with dangers and limitations. It is ironic that, in the caretaking dimension of the mothering or auntie roles, African American women have learned well how to take care of others, yet in intimate relationships they struggle to receive caring. Yes, there are possibilities for mutuality in mothering and sistering, but these are different from expressing sexuality and learning intimacy. Sexuality, where reciprocal relationships with another adult should develop, becomes an area in greatest need of healing. This chapter begins to look at the costs of brokenness due to the legacy of white sexual assault, to use Kelly Brown Douglas's term.

This chapter begins with a discussion of societal and domestic violence, then moves to sexual violence. AIDS is then discussed, followed by a section on the issues of politics and morality. I close the chapter looking for the hope of healing for African American women's sexualities. The conclusion of the chapter does not offer definitive solutions. I am exploring problems in this and the previous chapter; even these problem statements are tenuous and in need of the wider black community's — church folk, nonbelievers, intellectuals, grassroots workers, young, and old — protracted dialogue. What is certain is the need for healing.

Societal and Family Violence

The United States is a violent place to live. American-style violence is found in the number of guns, the death penalty, and road rage, as well as refusal to assist the neediest in society. We talk anti-abortion and pat ourselves on the collective back even as we wonder why the homeless won't just disappear. There are significant racist overtones in the nature of American societal violence. The social satirist Michael Moore is a white man who sardonically analyzes the American situation.

> You name the problem, the disease, the human suffering, or the abject misery visited upon millions, and I'll bet you ten bucks I can put a white face on it faster than you can name the members of 'N Sync. And yet when I turn on the news each night, what do I see again and again? *Black* men alleged to be killing, raping, mugging, stabbing, gangbanging, looting, rioting, selling drugs . . . It's odd that, despite the fact that most crimes are committed by whites, black faces are usually attached to what we think of as "crime."[1]

Although Moore uses satire to make his point, Jacqueline Battalora is much more direct as she writes: "The fact is that white privilege is not the result of something that any given white person requests. The presumption of the superiority of whiteness is for most white people largely not self-conscious, but rather is the product of taken-for-granted ways of seeing and behaviors that are learned and perpetuated through everyday behaviors."[2] Both Moore and Battalora indicate the recent scholarly area known as whiteness studies. Cutting across disciplines, whiteness studies is a slowly growing area of research where white people deconstruct the realities of the white race. To ignore the privilege of white Americans is to perpetuate violence on black and brown Americans. These researches are necessary if the health of the entire United States is considered. White privilege is intrinsic to the issue of societal violence.

Violence in the United States is so entrenched that it has become part of the culture, often experienced vicariously through movies, sports, and video games. From teen-slasher movies to hockey to voting someone off the island, Americans learn multiple forms of pain and rejection and call them entertainment. The violent culture in this country, with imperialistic influence, infects the health of other countries. The impact on the rest of the world of the American empire and its policies becomes a litany of self-service; American companies foist their defective products off on the poorest, weakest countries; American military training is provided for dictators in the name of making international "friends"; oppressive regimes receive billions in American dollars.

Even in the efforts to provide assistance to the poor or the ill in this country, violence is perpetrated. Cheryl Kirk-Duggan is a womanist ethicist who writes of American violence in efforts to help the neediest of society.

> We often want to fix people instead of empowering them. Such acts are acts of violence. We have a fixed way we want to relate to *those* people and we dare *them* to impede on our turf or to even think about challenging our authority base. We are often afraid that someone will find us out, that we really are not who we present ourselves to be. . . . Often those of us who claim to be liberal are actually Stalinist. We tend to name the oppressions that affect us and let the others go to the recycle bin of our minds. Here we do violence to our psyches and our spirits.[3]

The connections between the violence in American society at large and in black communities specifically are not accidental. When a violent society denies its own brutality, while creating a religious layer of lies to protect itself as it smashes the weaker members of the group, violence becomes a socially acceptable way of life. There are vindicationist statements in some black communities that blame black-on-black violence on the evil influence of white people, but this kind of thinking is too simplistic: we are all part of systems in which we live and work. Finding ways to name and correct the systemic injustices becomes the work of the whole community.

American societal violence is closely related to family and sexual violence. Black feminist Angela Davis named some dynamics of the relationships between societal and sexual violence a few years ago. The same links remain true today.

> The very same social conditions which spawn racist violence — the same social conditions which encourage attacks on workers, and the political posture which justifies U.S. intervention in Central America and aid to the apartheid government in South Africa — are the same forces which encourage sexual violence. Thus, sexual violence can never be completely eradicated until we have succeeded in affecting a whole range of radical social transformations in our country.[4]

Violence at home includes sibling aggression, child abuse, and spousal abuse. Violence, as used here, is meant in its widest form: physical, certainly, but the intangibles of emotional and mental abuse must be considered. The damage done to black people is not always visible to the eye, and we, like the rest of America, learn very effective ways of hurting each other without lifting a finger, such as emotional withholding or outright rejection. For a people who are not generally accepted by the rest of society, how much more weight might these carry when the rejection is also from family members? Considering sibling aggression is also important, because such hostility leads to isolation and weakening of economic strength when family members become competitive, living in resentment and anger. These forms of damage are often overlooked when considering black health issues. Some theorists insist that only physical damage can be statistically counted. Including the nonphysical forms of abuse is important for this study, where emphasis is given to relationships among black women and men. Emotional or mental abuse may seem invisible, but the results are seen in black families. I am not promoting some ideal image of "family" when I discuss the impact of violence on black families; that thinking leads back to the tendencies to blame African Americans for the state of our lives. Instead, I am recognizing the psychological and spiritual stressors that occur when a person is simultaneously segregated in society and separated from a significant personal support base.

Abuse of black children often eludes the eyes of community workers and neighbors who may suspect the child of being "bad." For instance, behavioral indicators of emotional abuse include habit disorders, delinquent or antisocial behavior, and destructiveness.[5] These symptoms can be misinterpreted because stereotypes of black people begin in childhood: we are often deemed flawed from birth. Without the drama of a broken arm or cigarette burn, the damage done to black children emotionally can easily be misjudged as no more than willfulness.

Child abuse is a contentious issue within African American communities because the goal of physical punishment in many African American communities is to protect children. Protection of African American children was and is a primary concern in black homes, as discussed in chapter 2. Correction was considered a form of protection with verbal and physical corrections by people who were the central caregivers. But what corrective actions might protect children today? "Spare the rod, spoil the child" is still preached in family, church, and neighborhood groupings. Many older people will say, "*We* were spanked as children, and it didn't hurt us." This statement implies that black people in past years had fewer problems than they do today, because they were physically punished. When asked to describe the "spankings," belts and green switches that raised welts or drew blood are the primary disciplinary tools listed. Some African Americans discuss the use of more extreme physical punishments by parents or guardians, such as being knocked down stairs or locked in closets. Viewing these childhood physical contacts with nostalgia indicates how the past punishments functioned for African American communities, as corrective action that ensured safety, in a sense. African American children were overly disciplined as a way to protect them in a world where they expected abuse by white people. On one hand, children were taught to remain silent and avoid attracting attention to themselves. At the same time, children were taught to expect life's experiences to be cruel. As such, punishment was intended as a survival method and character builder. Trying to apply methods that helped communities survive the overt impact of Jim Crow does not assist growth in a society where the rules have changed and racism is much more subtle. Using old methods in new times prepares black children to live in the past rather than move toward the future.

Another historically grounded form of protection was found in the dozens, the sometimes humorous language of insults, exchanged among members of the African American community. The dozens served protective functions as well. African American anger was not an acceptable response in American society. Indeed, in some business settings today, any African American who responds to injustice with anger is considered threatening. The dozens was a way to avoid internalizing anger, an inoculation for insults, intentional or not, by white people. The pattern of insults has come to serve another protective function, as word weapons in a hostile world. In urban settings in particular as black folk began to migrate to the North, the dozens established patterns of acceptable social communication among peers. One person's or family member's appearance — dress, walk, hair, or skin color — could become subject to another's loud, insulting, and usually public commentary. "You're so ugly that... " The response by the insulted person was supposed to snap back with an even more derogatory comment. The cleverness of the insult, the rhythm of the words, and the effectiveness in angering the other person were all part of playing the dozens. The dozens continues, given different names such as *snaps*. Some African American comedians, such as Richard Pryor and Wanda Sykes, have brought the language patterns of the clever insult into the general American public. Yet there is potential violence in this pattern of insulting one another, aiming hurtful words at perceived weaknesses in the emotional armor of the other person. The danger in the dozens was and is real: when an insult crosses the line of the tolerable, physical violence may be a response.

The violence between siblings in black families is sometimes part of correction and protection patterns as one child attempts to coerce the other into some behavior. In attempts to take responsibility for each other, to be "family," children may act out the coercive behavior patterns that they witness adults performing. If being "family" in American traditions encompasses patterns of violence, the values that underlie the behavior should be scrutinized in order to make changes.

Violence in African American communities has escalated beyond the concept of correction to protect. African American children become victims of abusive adults. On August 19, 2003, in Detroit, four children were shot by their father, three of whom died. By the date of that incident, twenty-six children had been killed in Detroit; seventeen of those deaths were from guns. Guns in African American communities contribute to a new depth of belief in violence to protect self against all others, just as children learn that the only sure protection one has is to respond with physical violence. Children learn the violence of words as well, whether the dozens or cursing. Enter junior high schools in many urban areas and listen to the language of the children, peppered with insults against "yo' mama" and colorful curses. Television and music, with so much explicitly violent content, teach young people a language of hate and death. These media productions also contain sexually explicit content, mixing sex with violence. African American women are portrayed as sex objects who are available to be exploited and pimped by African American men. These videos create an illusion of false sophistication among African American children who have sexual awareness beyond children of past years.

The media's influence has been practically inescapable as African American parents and guardians try to find seemingly safe things for children to do while the adults struggle to balance incomes that do not meet family needs. African American family groupings are asked to do more to protect their children from inner cities when they have less access to the wealth that eases the strains of child rearing. Television programs and video games become babysitters for many black parents. As a result, African American children planted in front of video screens are less physically active and obesity rates increase. African American children are generally more isolated from each other and the adults in their homes, with fewer after-school activities available in poorer neighborhoods. The daily burden on urban and poor school systems is great, with lower parental/guardian involvement, where teachers are sometimes forced into the role of surrogate parent. Governmental policies, exemplified by the "no child left behind" programs, leave reality out of consideration as school systems are required to do more with less. These policies layer another blanket of violence on African American children in poor areas as they suffer the consequences of selfish, short-sighted bureaucrats. Marc Morial, president of the National Urban League, named the realities of black inequalities in his keynote address at the national convention in July 2003. He stated:

> There's an equality gap in education, there's an equality gap in income, in wealth, in access to quality health care, and home ownership. There's an equality gap between African Americans and Whites when it comes to participating in the political process.... As Dr. Robert Hill says, "James Crow, Esquire" represents the new, sometimes not so obvious structural inequality that persists 40 years later.[6]

These dynamics — society, media, education, and language — are all part of African American domestic violence. Spousal abuse is generally given somewhat more public attention than other forms of domestic violence, yet all are interrelated. One reason that

spousal abuse is singled out is that abuser and victim can be identified by statisticians and social service workers. Unless child abuse
or sibling aggression become very physically obvious, they are too
easy to overlook and connect to assumptions about how violent
African Americans are. In addition, efforts to change the degree
of awareness of spousal abuse in black communities are complicated by the fact that it is so visible and accepted. Sometimes their
battering is excused by appeals to race loyalty: what black woman
would put a brother in jail? Spousal abuse, for African Americans,
includes all forms of domestic partners, whether or not the partnership is legally bound. Including multiple forms of committed
relationships reflects the span of ways African Americans understand themselves as "married," a concept often unencumbered by
legal definitions. Violence occurs in these committed relationships
into which African American women invest energy.

Some of the dimensions of African American spousal abuse were
outlined by Beth Richie, a black sociologist. Richie did an extensive
study of black women who were incarcerated on Riker's Island, in
New York City. Her findings point out neglected dimensions that
landed the women in prison, among which is the idea of "gender
entrapment." Black women expend effort to try to fulfill the published ideals of a woman's gender role, especially being supportive
of the men in their lives.

> The commitment to dominant ideology and indeed the emo-
> tional work and social pressure to conform to it deeply
> influenced the African American battered women's adult inti-
> mate relationships. They, like the white women, were highly
> influenced by the hegemonic assumptions about the appro-
> priate public and private roles for women, and their attempts
> to approximate these roles were rewarded intermittently by
> traditional relationships with men, praise from their families,
> admiration of their peers, and social status as a "real family."[7]

Even as the women attempted to live up to these roles and were
caught in battering cycles, the need to maintain the relationships
with the men became more important than their own safety. To

fail at maintaining the relationship, even ending it for their own or their children's health, would be socially humiliating. The socially perceived necessity of preserving relationships at any cost is one of the differences between African American and white women's experiences of spousal abuse.

> The sense of public failure and accompanying loss of social, community, and family status reinforced the private shame and guilt many of the African American battered women felt. Some of their families overtly blamed the women either for the abuse or for not being able to cope with it. Other African American battered women lost their jobs, were unable to adequately care for their children, and some became homeless. . . . Being a battered woman did not carry as much social stigma for the white women.[8]

At the conclusion of her study, Richie stated that these same women, under different circumstances, would have been successful in life because of the very same character traits that led them into prison. "Their strength, self-confidence, cultural and family loyalty, and the optimism that ultimately led to gender entrapment were potentially their greatest assets."[9] Working to define their identities consumed these women, particularly their concern for fulfilling a presumed, prescribed gender role, which stresses once again the link between race and domestic violence.

Richie's concept of gender entrapment can certainly be applied to African American women outside prison systems. Black women become trapped into believing that they must "get" a man and should do whatever is necessary to maintain the relationship, while the man, if he is black, is to be given preference in nearly all things. When entering a relationship with this mind-set, becoming a battering victim may be inevitable. Gender role expectations become forces driving many black women into abusive relationships.

There is potential for escalation of black domestic violence, particularly when African American women fight with the men who attack them. The fighting back is tied to childhood patterns and social class, where many black women learn to respond to physical violence with more violence. Law enforcement and social services personnel might confuse who is attacking whom and be willing to blame and prosecute the women for assault. However, the fighting is partially rooted in power struggles as men seek to control women and define their own manhood. This needs inclusion in analyses of black American dynamics of domestic violence.

The escalation of violence in black homes is a major health problem.

> The fact is, most of the time the face behind the gun, the knife, or the clenched fist is a familiar one. In 1990, more than half of all homicides nationwide were committed either by family members, friends, or acquaintances during a fight. And for us, the statistics are much more deadly: The rate of domestic homicides among African-Americans is eight times greater than that of whites. Among murdered Black women, two-thirds of the victims knew their killers; in more than four out of ten cases, the attacker was a family member.[10]

Sexual Violence

To hold a wider view of sexual violence, rape and child sexual abuse are not the only forms that need to be considered. The perceptions that shape African American women's sexuality are a form of sexual violence. The sexual experiences of African American women have been formed by historically developed ideas that continue into the present. African American women are depicted as sexual adventurers, unable to control their libidinous drives. These ideas are so ingrained into American society that black men and women buy into them. Black feminist Tricia Rose highlighted contemporary, intensive, economic reinforcement of these sexual stereotypes.

> Since the 1990s, after black popular culture emerged as the defining and highly profitable element in American youth culture, the visual exploitation of black women in music, video and film skyrocketed along with black music profits. For many black women artists — and women artists generally — being

sexually explicit in ways that mirror trite patriarchal sexual fantasies has remained the most reliably profitable motif. This explosion by black female performers simply represents the music and film industry's profiting from the long-standing sexual ideas about black women. . . . It does not represent, as some have argued, a new black feminism. . . . Many very sexually explicit artists, such as Lil' Kim, Trina, and Foxy Brown, reinforced both the history of black women's sexuality as deviant and the primary role of black women in male hip-hop music videos as exotic sexual playthings and strip-club dancers.[11]

Being defined as sexual objects is the first form of sexual violence that many African American girls and women experience. The images are reinforced through pornography, where black women are shown as beasts or slaves. One study cited black novelist/essayist Alice Walker's biting commentary: "Where white women are depicted in pornography as 'objects', Black women are depicted as animals."[12] In the same study on racism in pornography, the negative ways that other women of color or ethnicity — Asian, Jewish, and Arabic — is considered in addition to black women. The authors of that study expressed deep concern over the possibilities of changing these racist depictions.

> An important unanswered question is why the liberal and radical community, as well as people of color who are not part of this community, appear to be totally unconcerned about the racism in pornographic materials in contrast to their concern about other manifestations of racism, such as those in ads, literature, media, verbal statements and so on. . . . Unfortunately . . . the combination of sex and racism appears to blunt people's response to pornographic racism just as the combination of sex and violence appears to dull concern about the consequences of portraying violence in pornography.[13]

The sexual image of African American women is encouraged and supported today by African American men. Strip clubs have become very popular forms of entertainment for African American men, surprisingly for young men in particular, as another author states:

> The greater visibility and homage paid to strip clubs in Black popular culture, namely in rap videos and films like Ice Cube's *The Playas Club,* reflect real-life trends. Likewise, the growth of younger Black, single, twenty-something patrons has been observed by topless club owners, bartenders, and patrons themselves.... Both young men and young women realize that some men have decided to go to clubs rather than spending money and time dating. Whereas strip clubs were once the domain of married men, bachelor party send-offs, and so-called social misfits, there is now a new breed: those interested in women only as sexual objects.[14]

It is not that large a step to the act of rape from thinking of African American women as sexual objects. Rape is about power, the power of the aggressor over the one being raped. The ridiculous idea that African American women and girls are supposed to "be asking for it" by behavior, location, or appearance permeates the culture and its music. Most locations across the United States are dangerous places for black girls to grow up, dangerous because their sexuality becomes a target making them subject to attack.

The treatment of African American women as "hoochie mamas" or whores is an extension of the belief that the women want sexual activity, which includes the related belief that rough and painful intercourse is preferred. There are some negative biological interpretations of black men as well as women in the act of rape: the men are judged such sexual animals that they could not help themselves; black women are believed to want the act, even if they clearly say "no."

> As Black women, we are twice as likely to be raped as white women and less likely to report it. Many women never tell another soul that they've been raped. Rape is trivialized and ignored. So many women are afraid they won't be believed,

and if they are, they'll be blamed for doing something to pro-
voke the attack. . . . But despite slavery's legacy of rape, the sad
and ugly truth is that it is not only the white man whom we
need to fear. More often than not, it is Black men who rape
Black women. The rapist may be our father, husband, date, or
stranger, but in eight of every ten rapes of Black women, the
rapist's face will be Black.[15]

Bakari Kitwana wrote of the hip-hop generation and reported that
black male loyalty has intensified today. "Countless rap lyrics speak
of sharing women and placing one's 'boys' and/or money above
one's significant other."[16] African American women involved in the
dating scene now face the possibility of gang rape as male friends
"bond" over the women's bodies. At the same time, African American girls and women are also pressured into sex in order to prove
they are "good" women who are respectful of men's wishes. Gail
Elizabeth Wyatt is a black psychologist who connects the past of
enslavement and names contemporary violence in sexual coercion
of young black women.

> I see a slave's inability to control her own sexual decision mak-
> ing mirrored in any black girl's inability to make decisions that
> are in her own best interest. If she is more curious about expe-
> riencing sexual information or more determined to please her
> partner than she is about protecting herself, there are plenty
> of people who are ready to exploit her needs. I think about a
> slave's vulnerability when I consider the sexual abuse of any
> black girl, with its long-lasting effects and subsequent influ-
> ences on sexual risk taking. That child is captive, too. She has
> difficulties in exercising her control and self-confidence. With-
> out these skills, she will be unable to advocate for herself when
> she is challenged by partners who wish to overpower, pressure,
> coerce, or manipulate her into having sex.[17]

Besides rape, incest and child sexual abuse are other forms of
sexual violence to consider. Incest and child sexual abuse are becoming, slowly, more visible in African American communities.

For many black Americans, there has long been the belief that "those kinds of things" were always done in white communities, and that black people only started incestuous activities after integration and greater involvement with white people. Maya Angelou and Oprah Winfrey, in telling their own stories of incest, have been part of breaking the silences around these topics. Their and other women's willingness to tell their stories become new sources of tapping power.

Although there is some recognition today of the presence of child sexual abuse and incest in black communities, there is no evenhanded approach: concern for black boys' sexual well-being outweighs that of girls. This is selective fear, reflecting African American homophobia. Such selective concern also reflects the stereotype that an African American girl will have an easier time coping than a boy. This mentality ultimately pits one set of hurting community members against others. The issue of incest and child sexual abuse needs attention regarding all members of the African American community.

One researcher, writing as a survivor, related four stereotypes about African American girls that create societal and communal blindness toward their pain. The first stereotype is that incest is normal in black communities. "On the one hand, it is not supposed to exist in our communities, to any degree (or so they say). This brings about a reluctance to raise it as an issue. . . . It's almost considered normal by many inside and outside black communities."[18] The second stereotype is that African American girls and women can and should handle the pain, just like they handle all other pain; black women, after all, are strong enough to take anything. Third, there is a serious misconception about the idea of incest as a form of sex education.

> Some men do indeed regard the incest as a way of "christening" or teaching their daughters about sex . . . as aiding their daughter's rite of passage into womanhood; and because of this, feel no remorse for the act. . . . Oftentimes, sleeping arrangements in black families — the close proximity of bedrooms — leads

to a lack of restraint. Sometime, somehow this contributes to
a feeling that it can't be sinful or wrong.[19]

The fourth stereotype returns to the idea that African American
girls and women are sexual animals, so family members should feel
no guilt for doing what the girls want to do anyway. Each of these
beliefs is a form of violence and leads to expressions of violence.

Sexuality, for African American girls, is a difficult terrain to cross
into adulthood. Ignoring these dangers is not protection. Gail Wyatt
discussed the idea of "stolen women," like enslaved African women,
as a way of naming the dangers. "The woman who exaggerates or
avoids her sexuality and allows others to simplify or stigmatize it
eventually finds herself paying the unnecessary price of continued
sexual slavery as one more stolen woman."[20]

AIDS

Black women are at the highest risk for infection with the AIDS
virus. "In 2001, almost two-thirds of the women in the United
States who found out they had AIDS were black," one researcher
stated.[21] These numbers are higher in some individual states:
89 percent of all HIV/AIDS cases diagnosed in Louisiana are black
women.[22] "Statistics indicate that the most frequent mode of trans-
mission of the HIV virus to black women is through sexual contact
with black men who are intravenous drug users and/or gay or bisexual. This means that to fully understand the impact of AIDS
on black women, attention must be given to the politically charged
issue of sexuality."[23]

The media campaigns to bring the issues to the community's
attention have been ongoing: billboards, discussions on black char-
acters' situation comedies, and community center pamphlets. One
of the most hopeful campaigns has been through black churches.
"The Black Church Week of Prayer for the Healing of AIDS" is held
annually and at least brings the term "AIDS" into the church pews.
Part of the problem with the programs I have attended is the unwillingness to address issues of safe sex practices, homosexuality, and

bisexuality in black communities. The numbers of black women infected with AIDS demonstrates that the programs are still not reaching their target audiences.

Urban legends in black communities surround and prevent AIDS discussions.

> One study in the '90s by the Southern Christian Leadership Conference found that 54 percent of blacks thought H.I.V. testing was a trick to infect them with AIDS. In the early '90s, the rapper Kool Moe Dee and Spike Lee expressed concern that H.I.V. was part of a calculated campaign intended to rid the world of gay men and minorities, and as recently as 1999, Will Smith told Vanity Fair that "possibly AIDS was created as a result of biological-warfare testing."[24]

Discussions about AIDS are generally blocked by black community attitudes. When one takes care to listen, the stories of the pain of contracting AIDS are profound. One African American woman, discovering she was infected with the virus, confronted her male partner who callously responded: "Why not? We share everything else."

But the pain of African American women through the AIDS virus is not limited to contracting it. As sociologist Beth Richie points out, African American women are given responsibility for the health of family members.

> The culturally dictated gender role of most women in black families requires that they be responsible for the health and well-being of their children, husband or sexual partner. This means when family members become sick, black women care for them, usually alone. . . . It is exhausting and expensive, and black women usually carry the burden by themselves.[25]

AIDS infects and impacts too many African American women. The silence around AIDS is related to many of the issues already discussed: homophobia, heterosexism, and sexual roles handed to black women. Addressing the problems becomes one more area where power must be tapped.

Black Women and Sexual Politics

For African American women, domestic violence is linked to gender role expectations and sexual violence is linked to sexuality role expectations. Both forms of violence enforce views of racism, of single views of family structures, and of patriarchal (black or white) privilege. Both forms are intimately connected with the power to control African American women's bodies. Control of African American women's bodies through the use of sexuality is achieved on a very public level, particularly through moral judgments against the women. African American women are blamed as the evil sexual animals, the wicked creatures that have no impulse control when it comes to sex acts (unless they have been safely desexualized, like the historic figure of Mammy). Designations of wickedness and evil are the controlling lines in that stereotype, labeling promiscuousness by African American women as inherently immoral. There is another aspect to the moral judgment: African American women are deemed too stupid to know they are being used. This thinking presents African American women as genetically flawed in their capacity to act ethically, mentally incapable of learning the impulse control necessary for social functioning. In this stereotype, all African American women are in need of constant observation. These judgments against black women are widely applied and become part of the rationale for maintaining surveillance over African American women in all settings.

Combining sexuality and morality has been a powerful way to control African Americans in general, especially regarding their effectiveness and inclusion in American public life. This becomes an effective weapon to control and silence public dissent. So Jesse Jackson's presence, especially his political effectiveness, was practically erased from public view after revelations of his extramarital sexual life; there was no need to physically assassinate him. Sexuality is effectively used to control the public acceptance of one citizen by other American citizens. This practice of sexual character assassination has been effective against women of all groups from the country's founding. Extending the red letter A(dultery) or P(erversion) or H(omosexual) to male minorities and selected white males is a mere refinement of the process that has been done to black and white American women, thus keeping them contained.

These moral judgments are effective ways of silencing dissent against so-called social norms, even if those norms are oppressing the dissenters. But silence does not really protect any group in American society any more than it protects the victim of domestic violence; silence only serves to support the larger patterns of deception. Legal scholar and Asian feminist Mari Matsuda stated the danger of silence: "What I have learned from my own experience and from the message of the gay and lesbian community is that 'silence equals death.' It can affirmatively harm you."[26] Breaking silence is not just a matter of complaining, but of actively becoming aware of the history of creating the silences and stereotypes.

For African American women, considering the experiences of sexual slavery, of being "stolen women" in Gail Wyatt's terminology, the history that created the present moment needs much greater exploration and no silences. The reason is clearly stated by Tricia Rose. "If we continue to downplay the importance of these powerful histories and social forces, we will keep them alive; we will mask and sustain their impact on our lives. Intimate justice comes from our working through, not around, these histories."[27]

Because of the success of the political labeling processes and the insertion of the idea that the labels of African American women are "normal," political actions can be taken that enforce against defiance. For instance, sex education is getting blamed for promoting greater sexual activity among young people. Therefore, many legislators are suggesting the need to establish "abstinence only" programs as the only form of sex education in public schools.[28] This thinking is mirrored in black churches, where the efforts to make "good" African American girls is still a focus of too many Sunday schools. If homosexuality is impossible to discuss in black churches, sexuality is barely on the table. Gail Wyatt found that the black women she interviewed received as children no information at church about sex, because young children were considered asexual by pastoral staff. While there are teen programs against pregnancy and substance abuse, she found, there is no information given to define the process of becoming pregnant or addicted.[29] Yet even if churches considered sex education the right of the adults in a household, some discussion of the components needed for guiding children should be promoted. Instead, scare tactics and religious dictums are used to limit young people's choices. As an example, one black church has a program that teaches girls to talk about Jesus as their "boyfriend," and therefore any other male's sexual advances should be rebuffed (implying, "Because you wouldn't want to let your boyfriend down"). However, young people's hormones do not flare up based on the amount of information in their brains; ignorance will never lead to abstinence. The choice to teach abstinence over information in black churches and often in homes still centers on the belief of protecting black girls from racist misuse. As one author stated, there is lip service given to the female-protection tradition within black communities:

> The call for reverence and protection [of black girls and women] stems from a sincere concern for black women's psychic and physical safety; however, the pure and protected black woman of this vision will also be obligated to obey her protector — the black man. Nonetheless, many black women continue to be willing to accept the terms of this contract. The promise of patriarchal protection is certainly much better than the methodical abuse suffered by black women throughout much of their history in the New World. It also seems to offer a solution to the problems faced by so many heterosexual black women who find themselves struggling to raise families without the economic and emotional support of a male partner. Even many women who find themselves in abusive relationships would trade in physical and emotional violence for protection and reverence.[30]

Control of African American women's sexuality within black communities is politicized with the moral overtones of restrictions being good for African American women and, in fact, the entire black race. These controls are woven into issues of African American women's sexuality, becoming part of the overall oppressive structures that are in need of healing.

Where Is Hope?

African American women's sexual lives are health hazards because the negative constructions are part of the American consciousness. The white pathologizing of African American sexualities and relationships has been a continual process that began when Europeans first encountered black people. The negative identifications of black sexualities as deviant, animalistic, childlike, and so on, justified colonizing and controlling black bodies in the past. While less blatant today, colonialist control continues as institutions of education, health, science, law, and social services produce further studies to prove the inadequacies and pathologies of contemporary African Americans. As a consequence, African Americans have expended great amounts of energy trying to prove we are *not* like the stereotypes. Honest identification of the troubles that are piled onto African American women's sexualities has begun. Tricia Rose's 2003 book, *Longing to Tell: Black Women Talk about Sexuality and Intimacy*, which was cited earlier, is part of the naming process. Twenty African American women painfully and courageously discuss issues of sexuality in Rose's book. Yet, it is not merely disclosing current realities of sexuality that is needed, but recognition of the history that created the current situations.

> If we are to understand more fully the portraits of the women presented here, we must also know the history of black women in America and its legacies. We are all deeply shaped by our histories in this world; histories that have seeped into places many of us find it difficult and painful to go. The personal lives of these women who stepped out on faith — and all of our lives — are shaped by the legacies of racial slavery and the diffused but nonetheless entrenched ideas about black people's sexuality that grew from them.[31]

The need to name our realities, in light of history and stereo-types, further exposes the ways that African American sexuality is misnamed in the United States. We must recognize that there is a cultural bias in preferred American family and marriage structures and gender constructions. The bias is for white, middle-class, phys-ically able, nuclear families, and the matching heterosexual gender role constructions are established as normative. Any other possi-bilities are construed as deviant. We must recognize that there is a religious bias in preferred American family and marriage structures and gender role constructions. The white Anglo-Saxon Protestant views of marriage, family, and gender are blessed and fused to the cultural biases, creating religious mythology about what a good and, by implication, godly family and its members look like. As soon as African American families and marriages do not meet these sur-face descriptions, they are considered ungodly. While all societies define their norms as part of processes of socialization, the fact is that African Americans were not considered when the norms were constructed, except as deviant. During the creation of these normative views, African Americans were, first, enslaved, and later captured under legalized segregation. The 1954 *Brown v. Board of Education* decision of the Supreme Court that declared separate but equal an impossibility could not magically erase different social structures and values, divergent political views, or distinct religious perspectives. The Great Society programs of the 1960s, antipoverty programs, and affirmative action have not been enough to erase dif-ferences between black and white America because none of these governmental programs went far enough.

What has been needed is a true analysis of what is truly exis-tent in and among African American communities across different regions of the United States. Some museums of African American history give pieces of the analysis. Reports from the Urban League or the NAACP present other data for analysis. Occasional research from colleges and universities begins to scratch at the surface of missing data. Part of the problem with these analytical efforts is the stubborn insistence by many agencies and academics that these labors are no more than political correctness that is on the fringe of real American history or research. Those few studies still miss discussions of African American sexualities and gender role constructions. Few consider what a healthy African American family looks like outside the WASP norms.

The present challenge for African Americans is to locate ways to develop sex education that is appropriate for our children and families. Serious conversations about sex are needed in black communities. Churches may or may not take the lead, but they should not hinder the discussions.

Naming African American realities including social structures and institutions, telling our stories about sexuality, and researching the history that led to the stories are but beginnings of a longer process. They are markers of hope in the middle of the multiple health hazards that sexualities bring to African Americans. But in order to tap power, more is needed. Toinette Eugene, a womanist ethicist, has offered some of the deepest insights into what is needed for healing African American sexuality and spirituality. Her contributions are discussed in chapter 7 as part of the longer discussion of womanist theology.

One other sign of hope should be mentioned here before moving to the next chapter. Women have begun to work in coalition with each other, crossing color and class boundaries. Sexualities, in both healthy and unhealthy expressions, are important areas of mutual exploration with other women, especially those of the African Diaspora. There are also special connections with other first-world women who are being third-worlded at home — Latinas, Chicanas, immigrant women, poor women. As we explore our individual pains, we need to look to each other for shared strategies, thus tapping power on a larger scale. We must support each other in stating our own realities, which may contrast sharply with those of middle- through upper-class white Western women. Supporting each other is one way to sap the strength of efforts to colonize our bodies.

SIX

African American Women and White Health Institutions

Something occurs in addition to the medication, 'cause I don't think that medication heals. I think that's just one small piece of helping us move on that continuum, but the healing aspect is greater. So when I see repeaters, there's no healing there. Even when symptoms re-occur, the people that have had some healing experience it differently.... They've got tumors, but they've been healed. They feel they are at a point where healing has occurred. They die peaceful. It's a different level I think in terms of the healing. We don't begin to really touch that a lot in health, in Western medicine.

—P'Jazz, interviewed in Detroit, 1997

Based on previous chapters, several questions could be raised about why African Americans have not utilized or adapted to health care institutions in the United States. If love relationships are problems, why not use therapists and counselors? If African American families want to look like white families, why have they not? If health is an issue in black communities, why have they not utilized available resources? For African Americans it is not just a matter of finance. The relationship between African Americans and health care institutions is complex and filled with disconnections.

The opening quote is by an African American woman who has a doctorate in nursing. Many people in the United States believe that becoming knowledgeable of and part of the white world is all that it takes to "get over" cultural differences. P'Jazz's words emphasize

120

some of the differences between African American perspectives and those dominant health care institutions that control images of healing. Health care institutions have not been able to understand how African Americans think. These institutions have functioned in dominant Western ways, determining that all civilized people and all Americans must think as they think, which includes ideation that divides body and soul and emotion into discrete categories, gives preference to the objective rather than the subjective, and builds health care on a business relationship with the health care provider. What might be healing for African American women and men is left out of health institutions.

African Americans have been treated as bodies upon which to experiment when they have been permitted into white hospital settings. Excluded from the health institutions and treated inhumanely, it is no wonder that African Americans do not trust mainstream medical professionals. At the same time, African Americans have viewed health care institutions as markers, among others, of acceptance into white society: becoming a medical professional in the white world was partially a calling to help and sometimes a calling to the economic and status benefits not available among segregated black communities.

Chapter 6 turns very specifically to relationships between African American women and men and the health care professions. While other chapters considered aspects of health within African American personal relationships, this chapter traces another story, that of the relationships between African American women and health care institutions. African American women are part of the larger United States and, as such, have their own story to tell of relationships with the legitimated, professional healthcare system of dominant society.

These stories of African American women working for or trying to work their way into health care institutions are tales of attempts to care for families. Attempts to care for black communities are also part of the stories. Throughout family and community care, African American women held, and continue to hold, an unusual place amid barriers between white Americans and black health. This chapter looks at some of the dynamics of this complicated relationship.

Stories of black women and men and health professions of the past pave the way for understanding more about relationships of the present. The struggles from within African American communities to improve health conditions used different strategies. In the early twentieth century, National Negro Health Week emerged and attempted to link African Americans with health goals and concepts from white medical institutions. How African American women suffered as a result is addressed in this chapter. At the same time that Health Week occurred, African American women were activists for black health. The last two sections of chapter 6 explore black health care today and the continued efforts of African American women to find alternative health care utilizing communal health and healing.

Trying to Work in the System: The Story of the Office of Negro Health

How should African Americans stand in relation to health care institutions? This question has plagued black intellectuals in particular ways since the nineteenth century's Emancipation Proclamation. African-based folk methods may not have disappeared but were ignored on a political level: such thinking became something from which many black intellectual and political leaders tried to distance themselves, in large part to achieve the widest possible public acceptance of their methods. Trying to achieve acceptance by white Americans has always been a difficult task, because most white people retain prejudices against and ideas about the inhumanity of African Americans. After the failed attempts of the Reconstruction period, the systems of the United States deliberately excluded African Americans and expanded privilege to whites. In particular, beginning in the mid-1800s, the professionalization of medicine and medical practice in America slowly became more focused. By the late 1800s, with growing urbanization and shifting demographics, this professionalization took on new intensity spurred by various public health movements.

African American efforts to improve health conditions were founded on several streams of thought. As a matter of ethics, efforts were made to demonstrate that African Americans were fully human and as such deserved care, not the brutality of the formally organized Klan or the informal dehumanizing treatment from other white Americans. With this basic ethical issue, the struggles of community leaders to safeguard black bodies were ongoing. In an effort to improve health, attempts to tap into the white medical profession's resources for the black community's benefit were continuous. These processes were led by the Office of Negro Health, which began from the establishment of Negro Health Week in 1914 by Booker T. Washington. Ironically, African American women were relegated to the sidelines of these efforts, often becoming case studies for health problems. The use of African American women as examples of poor health care was not invented by Washington or his cohorts; such use was already existent through the South.

For instance, "in 1904 the city of Macon, Georgia, passed a law to require washerwomen to buy badges that 'resemble those kept on hand for the city's canines.' Health reformers and politicians in Macon initiated the licensing system in response to complaints made to the police about 'missing washerwomen and missing clothes.'"[1] Following the example of Macon, some city government officials in Atlanta proposed laws for control of washerwomen and cooks. Tuberculosis (TB) became a medium for "framing tensions in labor and race relations,"[2] with the playing ground again black women's bodies. TB was perceived as the disease carried by African American domestics, most of whom were women.

The punitive emphasis given to disciplining and scrutinizing disease victims was consistent with the tenor of the broader public health movement in the nation. Police forces became integral to nascent public health infrastructures and to the enforcement of standards of purity, sobriety, and health. Black citizens in particular were subjected to police intrusion in their homes in search of germs. Where the police left off, public health nurses and social workers took over in the surveillance of victims of TB. Both black and white poor women were subjected to invasions of their privacy under the pretext of health care.[3]

Booker T. Washington initiated Negro Health Week in 1914, and while it lasted until 1950, few women were ever in prominent leadership positions. Robert Moton is considered a cofounder of Negro Health Week, heading what was called the Negro Organization Society. Washington and Moton drew from the thinking of the Progressive Era in the early twentieth century. Following emancipation, there was a conviction held, most often by white people, that newly freed black people's overall health was inferior at best given that they were no longer covered by the dubious health care benefits of enslavement. "According to the physician E. T. Easley, the 'suddenly altered status [of the Negro] in the body politic has brought upon him many evils and he has shown himself notoriously incompetent to meet the issues of his new social relations.' "[4]

With the prevalent science of germ theory, it was generally held that white people in contact with sick black people were in jeopardy of contracting diseases. Through Washington's Negro Health Week campaign, the idea of "spreading the gospel of health" centered on environmental cleanliness and personal hygiene as preventives of disease.[5] Where black and white Americans came in contact was a key political focus for Washington. The most common interracial encounters were between African American women who were domestics and their white employers, moments where very segregated worlds overlapped intimately. African American women were represented as potential disease carriers. In 1914, Washington related:

> When food is being prepared, the Negro touches the white man's life; when food is being served, the Negro woman touches the white man's life; when children are being nursed, the Negro woman touches the white man's life. . . . It is mighty important, in the interest of our race as well as in the interest of the white race, that the Negro woman be taught cleanliness and the laws of health.[6]

While head of the Organization Society in 1926, Moton applied the identical concept of the germ-carrying black woman in his promotion of Negro Health Week. He related a caricaturish tale of a black washerwoman, Aunt Hannah, hired to take home a white family's wash. Aunt Hannah was informed by her employer not to take that week's laundry home since one of the children had scarlet fever; the employer did not want to risk spreading the disease. Aunt Hannah replied: "Laws, Honey, don't worry about having scarlet fever. I have three grandchildren, and the last one is peeling now."[7]

These indictments of African American women as disease carriers appealed to the self-interests of white communities and leaders, so that in eighteen years, by 1932, a kind of success was achieved. The National Negro Health Week campaign, at one time alleging the participation of over 10,000 communities, parlayed its efforts in 1932 into the Office of Negro Health Work as center of the National Negro Health Movement, funded under the United States Public Health Service.[8] The first issue of the *National Negro Health News* from the United States Public Health Service cited the "loss of employment and wages, with the attendant train of ills, weakening the integrity and morale of the home and family and imposing greatly increased burdens upon several welfare agencies."[9] The conference adopted the "virile charge, 'Health First — More than ever before, Carry On!'" Negro Health Week was offered as a program with which to carry on, with its track record in affecting African American health.

> The extensive voluntary and cooperative practice in observing the Health Week relates to the national program the largest number of persons and agencies possible in the community and develops a wholesome health consciousness and spirit of "playing the game" that expresses [itself] in concrete accomplishment, not only for the individual community, but for the colored population and the nation at large.[10]

Despite the political maneuverings to further the gospel of cleanliness, the success of any public health campaign still depended on the existing social institutions of the African American communities. Black midwives in Mississippi, who were part of their communities, "from 1920 to 1950 . . . helped to implement the modern public health care system in Mississippi and other southern states. . . . Midwives were unique among health workers in that they were simultaneously the targets and the purveyors of health reform."[11] Even though African American women were targeted as health risks, they carried forward the gospel of cleanliness.

By 1950, the federal government was ready to get out of the business of specifically black public health work. The crisis, some African American community leaders related, was over. They attempted to put the most positive spin possible on the cut in funding the Office of Negro Health, as stated in the final issue of the *National Negro Health News.*

> This last issue of the *National Negro Health News* marks the end of one phase and the beginning of a new and significant phase of a great national movement. Eighteen years ago there was a pressing need to focus attention on the particular health problems of the Negro and to concentrate efforts in a national Negro health movement. Today, we know that this movement has been successful . . . so successful that there is not the same urgency to emphasize separate needs. Rather the trend now is for all groups to work together for mutual welfare. The National Negro Health Week movement has helped materially to gain general acceptance of the idea that "health is everybody's business."[12]

These comments indicate a shift toward the hope of ending segregated social structures — in other words, hoping for full integration of African Americans into American society and values. Yet, racial segregation remained the law of the land for several years and the practice for many years following the 1954 *Brown v. Board of Education* decision that declared separate unequal.

The Office and its publications were ended in 1950. The hopes of the African American public health promoters for equal opportunity health care may never have been realized. Meanwhile,

African American women created their own streams of leadership and worked on behalf of the community's health, sometimes with Washington or other formal efforts, sometimes not.

African American Women's Historic Efforts to Affect Black Health

African American women, from their arrival in the American colonies, regularly took care of the health and well-being of their own and white families. These actions were informed by past, half-forgotten learnings from the African continent (African cognitive orientations). But the women's motivations in caring for communities and families were shaped by experiences of living in this country. This set up a conflict for both African American women and men about their status in America. That status was relatively clear before the end of formal enslavement; even free black people were held distant from true citizenship. But on January 1, 1863, the Emancipation Proclamation brought hope to the millions of African Americans for full acceptance in the United States. That motivation generally shaped the development of Negro Health Week as well as the work of African American women in churches or clubs. Historian Evelyn Brooks Higginbotham developed the concept of the "politics of respectability" in black Baptist women's social work in the South during the early twentieth century as a major motivation.

> Respectability demanded that every individual in the black community assume responsibility for behavioral self-regulation and self-improvement along moral, educational and economic lines. The goal was to distance oneself as far as possible from images perpetuated by racist stereotypes.... The Baptist women spoke as if ever-cognizant of the gaze of white America. ... There could be no laxity as far as sexual conduct, cleanliness, temperance, hard work and politeness were concerned. There could be no transgression of society's norms.[13]

The black Baptist women, through their church councils and schools, encouraged African Americans to adopt the cultural values of middle-class white Americans. The women published value-laden health and wellness pamphlets to assist in this effort: "Take a Bath First," "How to Dress," "How to Get Rid of Bed Bugs," "Ten Things the Negro Needs," and "Anti-Hanging Out Committee."[14] The politics of respectability, as Higginbotham frames it, takes in the contradictory strands of this thought. Being "American" meant black folks' acceptance of responsibility to fit in. At the same time, as part of the politics of respectability, the Baptist women worked for civil and human rights of African Americans. These works ranged widely, from protesting the legalized idea of "separate but equal" to fighting for education of women, to organizing black women workers.[15] Acute recognition of how social conditions affected African Americans was intrinsic to health issues of African American women's activism.

The issues around physical health deeply concerned African American women in their early organizing efforts. Lynching of black Americans was a serious crime; it became a way for whites to control black bodies. Lynching became a jarring note to the belief that black people would be acceptable as American citizens if they were appropriately respectable. Social organizer Ida B. Wells-Barnett provided passionate leadership in the early twentieth century in addressing what she termed "our national crime." Before her marriage, Ida B. Wells had a career as a journalist. The lynching of Thomas Moss, a close friend, brought the issue home to Wells. "[Wells] had been so stunned by the lynching that she had had to force herself to write a cogent editorial for her readers. In her ten years as a journalist, and in the nearly half-century of writing that followed, her columns on the Moss lynching were the most painful."[16] Years later, she continued to castigate those who would lynch black people and called the United States to live up to its self-proclaimed Christian character.

From 1882, in which year 52 were lynched, down to the present, lynching has been along the color line. Mob murder increased yearly until in 1892 more than 200 victims were lynched and statistics show that 3,284 men, women and children have been put to death in this quarter of a century.... Why is mob murder permitted by a Christian nation? ... The cowardly lyncher revels in murder, then seeks to shield himself from public execration by claiming devotion to [white] woman.[17]

Besides individual efforts, African American women often began formal and informal organizations for community health, drawing on networking skills that were learned in the black community. The black clubwomen's movement, with its slogan of "lifting as we climb," provided significant services for the wider community. The relationship of African American women with American society was highlighted by the work of the clubs, which was, as the idea of the politics of respectability indicated, layered with contradictions.

The primary goal of black women in organized clubs was full acceptance and acculturation into mainstream society. They accepted the American values of liberty, equality, and humanitarianism. The efforts of the black elite to gain equality in American society coincided with the emergence of the American doctrine that required minority ethnic groups to assimilate into the dominant group and repudiate their cultural heritage.... Believing that blacks had something to contribute to America's identity, black women struggled to preserve their history, institutions, and cultural heritage.[18]

Many of these clubs functioned through black churches, which were significant locations for social reform.

Despite Booker T. Washington's leadership on the issue of health, African American women did not follow his ideas blindly. Paula Giddings shed light on the relationship between Washington and African American clubwomen.

In many instances there was accommodation to Washington's ideas — and power — Black women also operated independently of his influence.... It was Washington's philosophy of eschewing equal political and social rights that the clubwomen rebelled against most vehemently. Whatever their views on interracial relationships, for example, clubwomen took a stand against the prohibition of interracial marriage. Their position was that such laws made Black women all the more vulnerable to sexual exploitation.[19]

The efforts of African American women on behalf of the health of black communities took various forms. Numerous black clubwomen and their organized activities were the funding sources for African American hospitals and medical education facilities at a time when segregated health care was most often the rule. For example, the Provident Hospital was established in Chicago in 1891, one of the first in the country operated by black people. The hospital was funded through the networks of African American women's donations, collected from bake sales or their own employment.[20]

Throughout the country, clubs or networks also funded and established homes that cared for other African American women in situations of need. Without families or a home, African American women were both vulnerable and disposable to white society. When working away from their homes, African American women encountered difficulties in finding places to stay. Any urban area where black people were grouping in order to find work and improve their lives brought issues of care to the forefront. At the turn of the twentieth century, several examples from the Detroit area over a ten-year span demonstrate this. The Phyllis Wheatley Home, established in 1901 by an "association of women," provided living space for older black women. The Christian Industrial Club, begun in 1909, established a home for working women. The Detroit Women's Council, begun in 1911, worked to furnish guidance and support for young black women arriving in the city without families.[21]

These stories from the early twentieth century give only hints into the past relationships of African Americans and white health institutions. They do point out the marginalized spaces to which African American women were assigned and the ways the women re-created their own identities and still provided leadership to black health concerns.

The stories of African American health at the beginning of the twenty-first century carry some of the themes and problems of the last century and are compounded by new relationships between the United States and African Americans. The past blends into the contemporary relationships between African Americans and the health care industry.

African Americans and the Health Care Industry

The relationships between black people and the health care industry have been referenced in several ways throughout this book, including the rejection of granny midwives, the ridicule of black women's mothering, and the lack of recognition of existing structures in black communities. More direct alienation of African Americans from health care systems has been brought about by the use of those industries of black bodies: fears of night doctors, "scientific" exhibition of Sarah Bartmann's body parts, and experiments on black women's living bodies, for example. While this book focuses on African American women, the realities of the gaps between entire African American communities and health care institutions provide another aspect of the context: African American women are part of webs of community relationships. Their lives are impacted by the lives of members of their communities and families.

The distancing of African Americans from the health care industry today has been thorough and effective. That negative effectiveness is evidenced by the current circumstances of African Americans' health and is compounded by the health care industry's inability to communicate with black communities. Messages of missed opportunities and lack of trust come through repeatedly.

An example of this is found in the current AIDS crisis, which is at a critical stage in African American communities. One group of researchers stated:

The majority (65 percent) of the children in the United States living with AIDS are African American, and among adolescents between the ages of 13 and 19, African Americans represent over sixty percent of reported cases. The infection rate among African American adults is equally alarming and surpassing cancer, heart disease, and homicide. HIV/AIDS ranks as the leading cause of death for African American adults between the ages of 25 and 44. in addition, African American elderly account for the majority of AIDS cases of individuals over the age of 55. Given these alarming statistics, *traditional messages about the messengers for the epidemic are not reaching the African American community. More effective strategies . . . are necessary.*[22]

The lack of effective, culturally significant strategies is evident from prevention to treatment throughout the health care system. For instance, in the case of drug and alcohol treatment, medical social worker Sheila Battle wrote:

Highly regarded twelve-step programs such as Alcoholics Anonymous cannot be as effective for blacks until such programs take into account the outlook and experiences of African-Americans. For example, the first step in AA requires alcoholics to admit they are powerless over liquor and that their lives have become unmanageable as a result of alcohol abuse. This is not an earth-shattering or cataclysmic revelation that would immediately propel a black alcoholic into treatment. Powerlessness has been a factor for most people of color all their lives.[23]

The inability to recognize the social differences between African Americans and white Americans is incorporated in the larger denial of the effects of racial discrimination on physical health. Researchers with the Program for Research on Black Americans at the University of Michigan are exposing and exploring the connection between racial discrimination and poor health, drawing from the sometimes contradictory results. Their work is difficult in a national climate that generally wants to ignore problems associated with racism. However, the research group could state: "Racial discrimination influences the physical health outcomes of black Americans in multiple pathways. . . . These stressors may also invoke intermediate physiologic responses such as elevated blood pressure, or more long term ramifications such as the development of various forms of cardiovascular disease."[24] African Americans would not be shocked by these findings.

The impact of racism encompasses mental health. Rising rates of suicide among African Americans led Alvin Poussaint and Amy Alexander to research and write about the issue. They found that much reporting of suicide rates is incomplete or misinterpreted, citing one example of a report in the *New York Times* that "speculated, with no research support, that middle-class black youths were killing themselves in greater numbers out of disillusionment with their 'new affluence.'"[25] Poussaint and Alexander's findings parallel those of other researchers:

> The persistent presence of racism, despite the significant legal, social, and political progress made during the last half of the twentieth century, has created a physiological risk for black people that is virtually unknown to white Americans. We call this posttraumatic slavery syndrome. Specifically, a culture of oppression, the byproduct of this nation's development, has taken a tremendous toll on the minds and bodies of black people. . . . We see the increasing rates of black suicide in the United States . . . as part and parcel of that oppression.[26]

While these disconnections from obtaining treatment and from culture-specific services continue, African Americans are still excluded from health care professions with the exceptions of nurses' aides or licensed practical nurses or orderlies, some of the most powerless positions in health institutions. If the gaps between service and communities are to be bridged, there must be greater communal involvement in health institutions, which might consequently lead to changes in the ways that these institutions are operated in black communities. But that is a line of discussion beyond the scope of this book. What is critical for discussion now are ways that black women are continuing to tap power in these alienating times. Following are two examples of African American women's continued efforts to tap power for community health.

African American Women: Seeking Health, Tapping Power

African American women's foci on improving health of the community have shifted. There is now a recognition that African American women must take care of themselves as well as the community. To begin a discussion of the support for health care that African American women provide today, an excerpt from a piece that circulated the Internet at the turn of the twenty-first century provides a forceful image.

> On August 15, 1999, at 11:55 p.m., while struggling with the reality of being a human instead of a myth, the strong black woman passed away.
>
> Medical sources say she died of natural causes, but those who knew her know she died from being silent when she should have been screaming, smiling when she should have been raging, from being sick and not wanting anyone to know because her pain might inconvenience them.
>
> She died from an overdose of other people clinging to her when she didn't even have energy for herself. She died from loving men who didn't love themselves and could only offer her a crippled reflection. She died from raising children alone and for not being able to do a complete job....
>
> And sometimes when she refused to die, when she just refused to give in she was killed by the lethal images of blonde hair, blue eyes and flat butts, rejected by the O.J.'s, the Quincy's & the Poitiers.
>
> Sometimes she was stomped to death by racism & sexism, executed by hi-tech ignorance while she carried the family in

her belly, the community on her head, and the race on her back![27]

This poetic excerpt indicates a new attitude on the part of many African American women who are, as the great civil rights activist Fannie Lou Hamer said, sick and tired of being sick and tired. This time is different from that of the Negro Health Week. Some of the differences are obvious: legal segregation has ended, African Americans hypothetically can fully participate in U.S. social and political worlds, and economic power is available in theory. Fulfillment of the promises of social participation or wealth still eludes most African Americans, and being black is still more complicated than advertised. Therefore, in spite of tiredness, African American women still function in a reality that is more complicated by continued pressures to give in to gender entrapment with its quasi-religious underpinnings. Even when African American women do try to break free from past constraints, the politics of respectability still exists in black communities, creating its own tensions.

Furthermore, African American women have their own health care issues and challenges. Dorothy Roberts is a law professor who presents this context for African American women's interactions with health care institutions: "The lack of a continuing relationship with a personal physician has a profound impact on Black women's encounters with the medical system. While most middle-class white women can negotiate health services with the help of a personal physician who is socially like them, most Black women must face complicated and impersonal medical institutions on their own."[28] Their own challenges and familial, communal tensions impact the health of African American women. An important source of information on health for black women from their own perspectives is found in two popular publications.

Two major African American women's magazines, *Essence* and *Heart and Soul*, have featured themes of health and healing. *Essence* magazine covers a wide range of topics of interest to African American women, including fashion, travel, and home decorating. While these seem typical women's magazine fare, the difference is that topics are approached from the perspectives of African Americans. Fashion articles feature clothes not found in predominantly white women's magazines, in bolder colors and African-styled patterns; travel features describe locations within the African Diaspora; home decorating sections will give information on black designers or African artifacts. Health and healing are covered in the widest sense: not merely physical or mental health, but spiritual, political, and economic health issues are addressed, with a focus on relationships. In other words, a wellness approach to African American women's health is taken. One article, "Turning Chaos into Calm," advised women how to reduce stress in their lives.[29] Another explored reasons that African American women do not insist that their partners use condoms during sexual intercourse.[30] The work in one black Southern town, Quincy, Florida, to fight the AIDS epidemic was featured in a different essay.[31]

Heart and Soul was directly focused on health issues that impact African American women, still taking a wider view than dry recitation of data. By spotlighting a variety of well-being issues that intersect with African American women's lives, the magazine was able to get messages with health data into women's hands. For example, the topics in the October 2002 issue ranged from a story about one woman's spiritual journey ("One Love, One Faith, Two Baptisms")[32] to an article on bargaining tips ("Let's Make a Deal")[33] to the stories of breast cancer survivors ("Spirit Warriors").[34] The more deliberate focus on health issues led the magazine to make the following statement at the beginning of each issue: "The information in *Heart and Soul* is meant to increase your knowledge of health development and disease prevention. Because everyone is different, the ideas expressed by physicians and researchers cannot be used to diagnose or treat individual health problems." This disclaimer did not distract from the importance of placing the health information into women's hands. The magazine stopped publication in December 2003.

Individual authors are also promoting African American women's health. Some of the authors adopt views that attempt to make connections with African-derived healing concepts. One of these authors with a large following of African American women is Queen Afua. Her biography states that she is "an initiate of the shrine of Ptah and Chief Priestess of Purification in the temple of Neb-Het, an ancient Afrakan order." Her religious affiliation, like that of other African American women, indicates a deliberate distance from Western religious thought.

Her book does not approach or consider health from any framework that could be considered parallel to that of Western medicine. Queen Afua's book, *Sacred Woman: A Guide to Healing the Feminine Body, Mind, and Spirit*, provides exactly what the title offers, a healing guide. The writing is based on what is called "Khamitic Nubian Philosophy" that is a form of Egyptology. God, in this view, is understood differently.

> The Khamites, my ancestors, believed that within the heavenly realm the presence of the Divine is reflected in the balanced worship of NTR — the Mother/Father Creator, where both aspects in one are given equal respect. By contrast, most present-day Western religions recognize only the male priest and worship only a male God in a heaven of male angels. In the ancient Afrakan spiritual tradition, there is deep respect for the Mother Creator and the female priestesses as well as for the Father Creator and the male priests.[35]

With this as part of the philosophy from which she writes, the need for women to take care of themselves becomes a sacred duty, caring for the sacred temple of the body that is indeed made in the Mother Creator's image. The womb becomes a focal point of the healing process she describes, a healing that will expand to the world. "When our wombs are restored through the steady, unrelenting transformation of our thoughts and our hearts and our blood, then and only then will the destiny of the earth rise again.... Lost women are women who are disconnected from their sacred center."[36] Queen Afua then presents a series of "gateways" with meditation, exercise, food, and bathing for women to reach holistic healing.

African American Women's Continued Activism
for Health

> *Ah! Do you know some of the early theologians who talk about*
> *illness being a separation from self, a separation from society?*
> *That kind of isolation, that kind of non-communal-ness, is a*
> *state of ill health that gets manifested in all kinds of ways. We*
> *talk about the whole mind-body dynamic. Like arthritis. The*
> *idea that the arthritic is trying to hold on to something and*
> *treatment needs to be letting go. I certainly believe in disease,*
> *I know that exists. . . . But I also believe that we, depending on*
> *how we care for ourselves, will determine our vulnerability.*
>   — FRANCES, interviewed in Detroit, 1996

African American women continue to be involved with efforts for
the healing of black communities. There are significant differences
from the days of the clubwomen: women today diverge from popular trends, as in the case of Queen Afua, perhaps understanding the
meanings of professionalized medicine, sometimes making their
own definitions. Woven into professional or traditional understandings of healing are their own, derived from a basis of spirituality
and faith.

Throughout this book at the beginnings of sections, I have quoted
members of the Detroit Metropolitan Black Women's Health Project whom I interviewed between 1995 and 1997. The words of
these women continue to inform me, and I continue to be affected
by the years of working with them. Their commitment to issues
that promote the health and well-being of the entire community
was inspiring. Parallel with womanist thought, the members of
the Detroit Project emphasized the need for connections between
community activists and academics, crossing class or status lines,
learning from each other, working with mutuality and respect.
These processes of working together for the good of the community are distinct from those in past years that emphasized the need
for black people to model their communities on those of white
people. The distances between black and white communities are
most often felt by black people. The 1960s were years of political

protests, and while a few African Americans economically bene-
fited from resulting social changes, there are still too many gaps.
African American women in the twenty-first century, unlike the
clubwomen of the last century, are generally more battle weary
and less credulous. The past years' developments in the United
States have proven their suspicions to be justified. So the "strong
black woman" myth becomes one more battleground: in this case,
African American women fight the beliefs and the communities
that enforce the ideas of our tough minds and bodies that are resilient enough to deal with anything. African American women
have learned to reach out to each other, an extension of being sister friends, in order to survive. The Detroit Metropolitan Black
Women's Health Project has provided such an informal linking
among African American women in this area. Their story is not
isolated.

In Cincinnati, Ohio, I met a group of African American women
students who used their campus residence, with the blessing of
the university they attended, to open "Jumba la Nia" or House of
Purpose. The university students mentored area high school students. Like all university students, the university women struggled
to finish their homework and other commitments, but deliberately
retained their connections to the African American community.
They were collaborators and partners with community folk, helping girls not much younger than they to deal with their growing
pains. College, for them, was not a step away from the community but recognition of a different bond. Both of these groups, the
Detroit Metropolitan Black Women's Health Project and Jumba la
Nia, support a view of healing that is beyond physical diagnoses.
Both groups' work emphasizes the importance of relationality. The
ability to be in relationship with each other is a central aspect of
healing, from an African American cultural perspective. Trust of
known persons with whom there is some form of relationship and
mutuality is an important facet of entering into a healing process.
Healing processes, again from an African American perspective, are
not merely about physical treatments and prognoses, but encompass the entire person and the community. Vulnerability to illness,

as Frances stated at the beginning of this section, can be created by isolation and "non-communal-ness."

While some African American women group together to work on issues of healing, others work alone. One woman I interviewed in Detroit in 2003 is Angela, who has opened two small residential treatment facilities for the mentally ill, many of whom are drug addicted. One facility houses women, one houses men. Angela characterized the population that Care House served. "They are the paranoid schizophrenics and the low-level manic depressives and the clinical depressives and anxiety disorders and things like that. What we do is, we take them and we try and reincorporate them into society. Most of our population is homeless when they come to us." The first work is getting the residents to regularly bathe, eat, and dress as they had not when they lived on the streets. Getting them into treatment for substance abuse is another task. Regular treatment, school, and employment are next steps.

Angela's motivation to become involved in this field is shaped by personal experience.

> I'm a recovering addict and I also have mental illness. I have anxiety disorder and I am clinically depressed. And I just believe . . . my mom raised me to believe that I can do anything. And I believed her, I didn't have good sense, I believed her. So they told me when I was young [at a local clinic] and they evaluated me, and they told my mom that I was retarded. And that I wouldn't finish the third grade. My mom was like "What?! You crazy! My baby is not retarded . . . she just bad!" so she wouldn't buy into it and she never treated me like that. Now I do have a learning disability where I can't learn like everybody else. Even now I have to read things, and then have to go back and read them again. But I'm not retarded.

Angela found a therapy program that helped her. She returned to school and received her degree in counseling. She found that many African Americans are misdiagnosed by systems that do not understand them. This is exacerbated in the treatment process because, she said, "The therapy that African Americans need is laughter, music, and art. We need positive stimulus. Because we're a beautiful people, we're creative."

Angela began Care House, feeling called by God to do so.

That's why God created us, for one another. To help, to love, to protect one another. That's the Great Commission.... And this is my ministry. It's my mess, it's my message, and it's my ministry. That's what brought me here, to Care House. It was inspired by God because I was working [at another home].... [When I left that job] I prayed, I didn't know how me and my kids were going to live.... That's how God is though. What God put you in, he already knows the outcome. And if you walking on faith, even though it seems like the wildest, most unconceivable thing to do, the risk factor is so high ... but he said "stay" and I did. I'm still here.

While some forms of the politics of respectability push African American women's lives, the questions we face are different than in the past. There is less belief in the willingness of white Americans to embrace black women. The endings of both affirmative action and welfare, in different ways, emphasize this unwillingness. The attempted silencing of Sister Souljah and Lani Guinier by the Clinton administration, touted as the friends of black folks, told black women that our ideas were barely acceptable. These uncomfortable distances from mainstream America can be to the advantage of African American women: we are far enough away to see the truth and free enough to state it.

Other questions need to be stated in this section. With all that faces African American women regarding our health and well-being, how do we tap into our power to answer the questions of relationships with others in the United States? How do we relate to systems that minimally want us or directly oppress us? Ultimately, how do we determine what is best for our health? These questions overlap with the next chapter's womanist analysis.

SEVEN

WOMANIST EXPLORATIONS

Healing means knowing myself enough to know when something's wrong. It means loving myself to give myself permission to do all the things I need to do to get well, which means rest, which means crying, which means writing, which means people to hug me, which means access to the foods and herbs which help me balance myself, which means I don't have to kill another thing to stay alive, which means I want to live in a symbiotic relationship with the earth. It means acknowledging everything I know about black female religion. Healing means learning.   — LISA, interviewed in Detroit, 1996

The preceding pages lead to this point of reflection from a womanist theological perspective on the very meaning of health and healing and spirituality in African American women's lives. Embodied spirituality is both sensible and important in the context of African American women's lives. Such spirituality is sensible because it provides a survival mechanism in the face of repeated attacks. Embodied spirituality is important because it continues an African-derived sense of body and soul connectedness, which then imbues the strength to counter negative social judgments of African American women's bodies and lives. This embodied spirituality is not secretive but is expressed in daily life; it becomes a structure for understanding all life. Applied in the same holistic frame, embodied spirituality is expressed in relationships.

Womanist ethicist Toinette Eugene described three principles for embodied relationships. These principles directly counter negative social structures and become sources for healing in womanist terms.

> It is in the context of black relationships embodying a common vision of a transformed society that runs counter to the culture of domination, where we find the convergence of race, gender and sexuality that is liberating. . . . It is in the context of black relationships of deep commitment and attachment to one another, running counter to the culture of alienation, that we find the healing convergence of race, gender and sexuality. . . . It is in the context of black relationships formed and affirmed in the black family, the black community and the Black Church, running counter to the culture of despair, where we find the convergence of race, gender and sexuality that guides us with our past and calls us into the future of justice and sustained hope.[1]

It might be better stated that African American women's embodied spirituality has the potential to heal, and in that sense, has not been tapped for the power that it can yield. Part of the reason that the power in such a holistic spirituality is denied is that society continues to negate the lives that it seeks to control. In the same way, African American women's bodies become sites of contention because we live in a society that hopes to simultaneously ignore and still make use of those same bodies. However, African American women expend a great deal of energy resisting the ways that their selves are demeaned by American society. Here is where embodied spirituality enters because it serves as culture-based religiosity. This religiosity is not always related to a specific denomination, and freely draws from multiple denominations. The process of making sense of life through faith is an important religious quest that African American women undertake. Reflecting on life with eyes of faith is not pain-free. In fact, many African American women are broken by the negative experiences of life while other women buy into the limitations that society pronounces as normative. Yet, the hope for healing that Eugene's principles of embodied relationships point to have been viewed in the stories of African American women as mamas, aunties, grannies, and girlfriends; in these, the ability to create something new by tapping the power of embodied spirituality is enacted.

This chapter explores three themes that are part of African American women's religious works of tapping power: defining God and self in new ways, holding on to positive spirituality, and developing holistic resistance.

God in African American Women's Lives

African American women consistently define God in ways that assist in redefining and protecting themselves. God is generosity and kindness, which is known through God's unbiased acceptance of who the women are, regardless of where they have been in life. God is understood as mutually defining African American women as good, actively standing against negative social definitions and norms. Therefore, God stands *against* society's limits and *for* justice for women, their families, and communities. This justice-focused God actively promotes righteousness and calls African American women to participate in creating goodness in society.

This belief in a personal, interactive Divine Being brings God into relationship with African American women. This understanding of God emphasizes the idea of relationality, a non-Western concept that stresses the community over the individual. Mama, auntie, and granny are facets of this concept, which stands against the rugged individual touted by the American popular culture. African American women are called to work for justice on behalf of the community, as part of their personal expression of being in relationship with God. Knowing how to act for justice in communities is not simple. One reason is that justice is defined differently at different moments over time: what the clubwomen understood as acting justly would not fit a twenty-first-century framework, yet there are connections. The definitions of justice upheld by African American women often stand against those of American society. Like the stories of many of the women in this book, the processes of defining justice became situations of countering the wisdom of

American society. Learning to give voice to the definition of justice for any time period for many black women is related to giving voice to the power of God. Sojourner Truth's nineteenth-century arguments against enslavement and for women's suffrage still inspire African American women today. Tapping into God's justice is one aspect of African American women learning how to tap power.

God is power to be tapped as part of the relationship between God's self and women. In this relationship, healing of any ills becomes possible through faith. I interviewed Linda (in Detroit in 2003), who defined God as active and powerful. She had a certainty about her faith in this God who could accomplish anything, even against impossible odds. "If you put 'unconquerable' in big letters . . . by the time you could spell out the word . . . by the time you would get to the end, it's accomplished." She told of being healed of the desire to smoke cigarettes. Her son had nagged her, why didn't she stop smoking? He finally challenged her on the basis of faith.

> He says, "Mom, if God was so good, why don't you ask him to make you stop smoking those cigarettes?" I said, "Oh I'll do that. . . . " I worked at night and I prayed about it before I went to work. "God, I want to stop smoking cigarettes, help me." That night — I worked at a transitioning house — I would go outside with my clients in the backyard. So there we are, a beautiful summer in Colorado, and I'm smoking like I always do and then it dawned on me what I had said. And I told one of my clients, "I said I was not going to smoke. I'm going back inside." I went to my desk . . . and [took out paper] and I wrote. . . . "Lord, take the taste of nicotine from me." That was the last time I had a cigarette. I never had the desire to have one, in nine years now.

One of the women I interviewed is Denise (in Detroit, 2003), who stressed God as relational. Denise talked about her own experiences of coming to faith and knowing God through the faith healing. Denise attended a Sunday morning service. She had been in a car accident some months earlier that left shards of glass in her eyes. The glass would come to the surface occasionally. That Sunday morning, one of the pieces of glass was beginning to come to the surface. Following the service, the pastor laid hands on her, despite her objections. By the time she got home, the glass was gone. Later the same minister visited her in her home at the time her daughter had chicken pox. The minister laid hands on the daughter, and the following morning the rash was gone. She understood these healings no longer as mere coincidence but as God's actions. These healings happened at a time that Denise was in a journey toward conversion. Denise said that she responded, "Okay, if this is how you convert folks, then You got my attention now." She said that she had seen the actions of God in other people's lives, and watched "where they have been able not just to obtain things but their relationship changed because they now understood that it was a God that they could talk to, that they could reach, and it was a God that they could touch and they didn't have to go through somebody else." Two physical healings became opportunities for her to understand more about being in relationship with God. Denise talked about who God is in relationship with her.

> I have had so many encounters. I could rattle on for hours in terms of the things that I know that God has done in my life, things where I have seen His hand protect me from hurt....People say, "God drew you." No, I don't think he courted me that way. I think God has always just been there and said, "Well, I'll move for you." And it's not just material things. It's the feeling of well-being when you walk through your day and you are not looking over your shoulder.

Denise is a police officer in the city of Detroit. Her faith enters into her work life.

> When I get dressed for work, I know, when I put that vest on, when I put that blue uniform on, and put that shield on, I become a moving target. And I understand that, but there is a different sense of being. I'm not stupid, I'm not saying that I'm invincible to think that I can just walk out there and bullets

just, you know, bounce off of me. No, it's not like that. It's just I don't fear death anymore. I face the fact that when I leave here, there is a better place.

These two women's stories are not unusual. The connections between faith and healing, between God and community, and between members of the community are deeply etched in black cultures and are expressed in ways that health and healing are understood. A book that presents testimonies of healings and faith interspersed with original artwork is *On the Other Side.*[2] The author and artist, Alita Anderson, offers the oral accounts and her paintings of African American women and men and the ways that they come to understand healing in their lives. The connections between people and between the person being healed and God permeate these stories, accentuating the importance of relationality in black mind-sets. There is much that the institutional medical professions do not understand or recognize about the links between healing and relationality, creating gaps in the ability for institutional service to black communities. In spite of these gaps, African American women, from the base of their communities, find ways to strengthen their spirituality in order to meet hard times.

Spirituality for Impossible Times

African American women find ways to redefine themselves in positive ways through their active, interactive spirituality. Simultaneously, African American women find ways to define God in ways to support these self-apprehensions. Womanist theologian Delores Williams's discussion of Hagar provides insight into this God-and-African-American-women connection.

Williams foregrounds the biblical story of Hagar as central to African American women's experiences.[3] Hagar's story (Genesis 16:1–16; 21:1–21) resonates with many African American women. Hagar is the slave of Sarai, Abram's wife. Abram has been promised that God will make of him a great nation, but Sarai is barren. Sarai gives her slave, Hagar, to Abram. Hagar conceives and has a son, Ishmael. Womanist biblical scholar Renita Weems cautions: "It would not be totally fair to make the Old Testament story of Hagar and Sarai carry all the weight of the history of race relationships in the modern world. Yet the similarities between the biblical story and the relation of relationships across racial lines among women today are undeniable."[4] But the most salient feature of the story for African American women is Hagar's time in the wilderness. In her first experience, Hagar escapes from Sarai and Abram into the desert and encounters an angel of God who sends her back to bondage. Hagar marveled that she had seen and spoken with God. In the second experience, Hagar and her son are thrown out of Abraham's camp after Sarah bears a son. In the desert, fearful for her child's life, Hagar waited for death. Instead, she heard from God again, who told her not to be afraid and showed her water so that she and her son could live.

Like Hagar, because her story was about impossibilities as well, African American women learn "Hagar" spirituality. Spirituality becomes a way of surviving in the midst of impossible situations. The general rejection of American society, the experiences of being unloved while still under surveillance for the slightest misstep is the wilderness experience that African American women know as well, Delores Williams points out. African American women learn desert survival skills with a sense of being in relationship with a personal God who guides and teaches: flourishing in the desert places becomes possible.

In spite of these survival and growth skills, of learning how to be mama and auntie, the fact is that African American women can and do participate in self-destructive behaviors: despair is always a temptation. As discussed throughout this book, African American women can become entrapped in social definitions of their own limitations. Patricia J. Williams, a law professor at Harvard, developed the idea of spirit murder, which is "a disregard for others whose lives qualitatively depend on our regard" and includes "racism, cultural obliteration, prostitution, abandonment of the elderly and the homeless, and genocide."[5]

Spirit murder can be seen as the end result of the spirit sickness which Toinette Eugene described. Her definitions of sexist and spiritualistic dualism provide a diagnosis that sheds light on this discussion.

> *Sexist dualism* refers to the systematic subordination of women in church and society, within interpersonal relationships between males and females, as well as within linguistic patterns and thought formulations by which women are dominated.... *Spiritualistic dualism* has its roots in the body-spirit dichotomy abounding in white western philosophy and culture introduced at the beginning of the Christian era.[6]

A disembodied spirituality is the consequence of these dualisms and creates what Eugene calls "a central limitation in the development of black love."[7] It is damaging for African American women to accept this idea of disembodied spirituality because it closes the door against learning the lessons of the wilderness and becomes a part of adopting the self-hatred which society implies that black women deserve.

Retention of culturally based spirituality is not divisive of African Americans from other Americans. Many people, black and white, hope for the day that all people are truly welcomed into American life. The rejection of spiritualities that derive from cultures other than Western European does not build a better American citizen; such rejection is part of patterns of spirit murder. Spirit murder demands resistance, not compliance. African American women's abilities to resist become a spiritual journey and are part of a spiritual maturation process. Tapping the power of wilderness skills becomes a spiritual resource for a people disregarded within American society.

Elaine Brown Crawford terms this "womanist hope," which is

> the embodied hope of African American women that moves the personal, social, and political cogs in the wheels of the transformative process. Embodied hope is a lived witness that

discerns God's presence in the experience of African American women. Womanist hope is the bridge constructed with theological belief and social justice that binds and strengthens the community. This bridge of hope welcomes the Hagars, the Sojourners [Truth], and the unnamed women.[8]

"And Your Daughters Shall Prophesy"

Like other human beings, African American women aim for wholeness, despite the challenges of living in the United States. Health is not divorced from cultural frameworks: for the majority of African American women, finding a way to heal the heart becomes embedded into the culture. Byllye Avery, founder of the National Black Women's Health Project, wrote: "There are many ways to heal. Tears and laughter are important parts of the healing process. When we connect to our painful feelings from past hurts, this pain causes us to cry, and we begin to heal. Laughing about something that was embarrassing or anxiety-provoking in the past provides a feeling of relief."[9] Certainly the engagement of emotions in healing processes is not exclusive to African American women. But emotions that spring from the combinations of racism, heterosexism, gendered role constrictions, classism, and the myriad forms of spirit murder designed just for black women mean that there are distinctive complications in black healing processes. These complications involve women and men in African American communities where images of unending black strength impact health realities.

Many black Americans have internalized the belief that they are exceptionally strong, and over many decades have come to view themselves as being somehow inured to emotional stress. In the real world, African-Americans do exhibit an inner fortitude of the kind often found among people who are relegated to outsider status in a given society. . . . However, the responses of African-Americans to social pressure from racism and discrimination today are markedly different from those of their forbears. Developing and using the interpersonal and emotional skills that a black person needs to safely and productively make his or her way thought life in postmodern American can be a difficult task.[10]

The similar experiences of attempted spirit murder—of African American men and women who are disregarded—can become the basis of building strategic alliances that can create positive social changes that bring healing. Community building is part of that desire to catalyze healing. From the black clubwomen in the late nineteenth century to the National Black Women's Health Project in the late twentieth century, African American women have attempted to use organizations to provide health and care for the community, as well as impact social structures. Individual African American women have attempted to do the same thing, ranging from Ida Wells-Barnett's decades of work to end black lynchings to Angela's newly begun Care House to address homelessness and mental health in the black community (discussed in the last chapter). These efforts to heal physical conditions cannot be separated from spiritual concerns. The works these women have accomplished give particular care to those people whom white American society disregards as part of the processes of spirit murder. Such physical and emotional healing work is deeply spiritual.

Yet too often black churches take this work for granted. Churches should be the first to recognize the importance of African American women's communal healing work, especially in its distinctive embodied spirituality. Instead, too many churches in black communities are centered on enforcement of gender roles for "good" women rather than learning the lessons from the women's healing work. However, churches still constitute significant centers for African American women's healing work. As in the not-too-distant Jim Crow past, women are able to network with other African American women, learn organizational skills as needed, and receive some form of personal regard in an otherwise hostile world. African American women find, in these church settings, that they can tap into, and thereby become aware of, their own power. Womanist sociologist Cheryl Townsend Gilkes points to this in her research on black women in churches. "Black churchwomen approach their churches and communities with the understanding that they matter and they are indeed indispensable. When their voices and authority are challenged within their churches, they sometimes respond, 'If it wasn't for the women, you wouldn't have a church.'"[11]

Gilkes extends recognition of the importance of women building and healing community to the works of other women of color.

Most women of color are trapped in the worst and dirtiest sectors of the female labor market, providing the sole support of their families or supplementing the wages of their husbands, who are similarly trapped in male markets. Their families are not accorded the institutional and ideological supports that benefit white families. Additionally African American, Asian, Latina, and Native American women also do community work. They find their historical role organized around the nurturance and defense and advancement of an oppressed public family. Women in a variety of community settings now and historically have demonstrated that it is safe to parallel the oft-repeated statement of African-American church women . . . to say "If it wasn't for women of color, African-American, Asian, Latino, and native peoples would have far fewer alternatives and resources to maintain themselves and challenge a hostile social system."[12]

These linkages have tremendous potential for strategic alliances.

Yet discussions of African American women's community work call up allusions that all their efforts are aimed toward fulfilling the American myth of success. While very few would refuse the economic comforts that the United States has to offer, self-serving greed is seldom the single motivation that drives African American women. Instead, success may have another measure, one that is connected with family and community well-being. In the push to build communities, there is much confusion among most African Americans because there are few mentors. People like Angela at Care House may experience isolation in their efforts. The assurance of her faith in a loving God may be enough to hold her to the vision of a healed society. But beyond black communities, persistent media images suggest that safety is secured only with excessive amounts of money.

A dilemma results in thinking through the goal of communal healing in the twenty-first century. It becomes clear that healing in order to mirror mainstream American society is not healthy; problems regarding women, sexism, heterosexism, and family are clearly exhibited in white communities. There is no utopia to be found there, as the clubwomen discovered. America has never known a healthy society. The flaws that divided one community from another and privileged a small group were written into the Constitution. An additional dilemma is posed for African American women by the question "healing for what?" Thinking through this question can lead to a recognition that there is need to reenvision community and reconfigure family and nation, which entails giving up the thrill of violence and the pseudo-power of domination. For these tasks, imagination is needed.

The esteem of the community needs an end to spirit murder: self-esteem is not a luxury. The holiness of individuals must be embodied as a means to achieve a communal wholeness. For Christians, this is no less than belief in the resurrection of Jesus — and the promise of our own resurrection. Salvation cannot happen to select communities, in a vacuum. This is the wisdom of African American women who work for healing. Healing is a salvific task. African American women, along with other women of color who have been involved in tasks of communal healing, have some basic gifts that can educate those who never had or have lost the rich meaning of their own humanity within the global community. The creativity that African American women have used to reimagine themselves, to construct new relationships, to learn some ways to care for each other, while holding spirituality in their bodies and using sassy language to provide protection — these gifts can provide hope and leadership for new visions. Here is the heart of the healing wisdom of African American women.

NOTES

Preface

1. *Vital Signs* 11, no. 3 (July–September 1995): 3.

2. Michele Wallace, "Variations on Negation and the Heresy of Black Feminist Creativity," in *Reading Black, Reading Feminist*, ed. Henry Louis Gates (New York: Meridian Books, 1990), 54.

3. Ibid., 62.

4. Alice Walker, *In Search of Our Mothers' Gardens* (San Diego: Harcourt Brace Jovanovich, 1983), xi–xii.

Chapter 1 / Prelude to Tapping Power: Juggling Acts

1. Walter Johnson, *Soul by Soul: Life inside the Antebellum Slave Market* (Cambridge: Harvard University Press, 1999), 20, 21.

2. Ibid., 118.

3. Ibid., 153.

4. Ibid., 20.

5. Sharla Fett, *Working Cures: Healing, Health, and Power on Southern Slave Plantations* (Chapel Hill: University of North Carolina Press, 2002), 4.

6. Harold Jackson, "Race and the Politics of Medicine in Nineteenth-Century Georgia," in *Bones in the Basement: Postmortem Racism in Nineteenth-Century Medical Training*, ed. Robert L. Blakely and Judith M. Harrington (Washington, D.C.: Smithsonian Institution Press, 1997), 188.

7. Ibid., 189.

8. M. Shawn Copeland, "Body, Representation, and Black Religious Discourse," in *Postcolonialism, Feminism, and Religious Discourse*, ed. Laura E. Donaldson and Kwok Pui-Lan (New York: Routledge, 2002), 184.

9. Cheryl Mwaria, "Biomedical Ethics, Gender, and Ethnicity," in *Black Feminist Anthropology: Theory, Politics, Praxis, and Poetics*, ed. Irma McClaurin (New Brunswick, N.J.: Rutgers University Press, 2001), 198–99.

10. Ibid., 199–200.

11. Richard Meckel, "Racialism and Infant Death: Late Nineteenth- and Early Twentieth-Century Socio-medical Discourse on African American Infant Mortality," in *Migrants, Minorities and Health: Historical and Contemporary Studies*, ed. Lara Marks and Michael Worboys (London: Routledge, 1997), 71.

12. Jackson, "Race and the Politics of Medicine," 194.

13. Grace Elizabeth Hale, *Making Whiteness: The Culture of Segregation in the South, 1890–1940* (New York: Vintage Books, 1998), 203.

14. Copeland, "Body, Representation, and Black Religious Discourse," 188.

15. Alvin F. Poussaint and Amy Alexander, *Lay My Burden Down: Unraveling Suicide and the Mental Health Crisis among African-Americans* (Boston: Beacon Press, 2000), 15.

16. Adrienne Davis, "'Don't Let Nobody Bother Yo' Principle': The Sexual Economy of American Slavery," in *Sister Circle: Black Women and Work*, ed. Sharon Harley (New Brunswick, N.J.: Rutgers University Press, 2002), 121.

17. Sarah E. Chinn, *Technology and the Logic of American Racism: A Cultural History of the Body as Evidence* (London: Continuum, 2000), 6.

18. The 2000 Census was the first to use this black or combination accounting system. 54.5 percent of the 1.8 million who chose black in combination with another ethnic group are under age eighteen. Source: U.S. Census Bureau.

19. Retrieved from www.census.gov/Press-Release/www.2002/cb02ff01.html.

20. U.S. Census Bureau, "Facts and Features, African American History Month: February 2002," released January 17, 2002.

21. National Center for Health Statistics, United States, 2002 with Chartbook on Trends in the Health of Americans (Hyattsville, Md., 2002), 188. White women's cancer survival rate is shown as 63.3, African American women's as 49.9.

22. Ibid., 161.

23. Ibid., 182.

24. Jacqueline Battalora, "The Workings of an Ideology," in *Gender, Ethnicity, and Religion: Views from the Other Side*, ed. Rosemary Radford Ruether (Minneapolis: Fortress Press, 2002), 8.

25. Carl V. Hill, Rashid S. Njai, Harold W. Neighbors, David R. Williams, and James S. Jackson, "Racial Discrimination and the Physical Health of Black Americans: Review of the Literature on Community Studies of Race and Health," *African American Research Perspectives* 9, no. 1 (Winter 2003): 12.

26. Ann L. Riley, "Health and Self-Esteem among African Americans," *African American Research Perspectives* 9, no. 1 (Winter 2003): 158; emphasis added.

27. National Center for Health Statistics, United States, 2002 with Chartbook on Trends in the Health of Americans, 179–80.

28. Kelly Brown Douglas, *Sexuality and the Black Church: A Womanist Perspective* (Maryknoll, N.Y.: Orbis Books, 1999). See her chap. 3, "The Legacy of White Sexual Assault," 63–86.

29. Ibid., 67.

30. Poussaint and Alexander, *Lay My Burden Down*, 16.

31. "The National Survey of American Life and the World Mental Health 2000 Study," in *Program for Research on Black Americans and African American Mental Health Research Program* 6, no. 2 (Fall 2002): 2.

32. Terry L. Mills and Yvonne J. Combs, "Environmental Factors, Income Inequity, and Health Disparity: Emerging Research and Policy Implications for Black Americans," *African American Research Perspectives* 8, no. 2 (Fall 2002): 30.

33. Myron Orfield, *Detroit Metropolitics: A Regional Agenda for Community and Stability*, Report to the Archdiocese of Detroit, January 1999, Detroit, Michigan, 5.

34. Ibid., 18.

35. U.S. Department of Labor, Bureau of Labor Statistics, December 2002.

36. *The Detroit News*, Sunday, December 22, 2002, 1C.

37. Byllye Avery, *An Altar of Words: Wisdom, Comfort, and Inspiration for African American Women* (New York: Broadway Books, 1998), 8.

38. Vincent L. Wimbush, ed., *African Americans and the Bible: Sacred Texts and Social Textures* (New York: Continuum, 2001).

39. Joyce West Stevens, *Smart and Sassy: The Strengths of Inner-City Black Girls* (New York: Oxford University Press, 2002), 84.

40. M. Shawn Copeland, "Wading through Many Sorrows: Toward a Theology of Suffering in Womanist Perspective," in *A Troubling in My Soul: Womanist Perspectives on Evil and Suffering*, ed. Emilie M. Townes (Maryknoll, N.Y.: Orbis Books, 1993), 118.

41. Va Lecia L. Adams and Teresa D. LaFromboise, "Self-in-Relation Theory and African American Female Development," in *The Intersection of Race, Class, and Gender in Multicultural Counseling*, ed. Donald B. Pope-Davis and Hardin L. K. Coleman (Thousand Oaks, Calif.: Sage, 2001), 30.

42. Delores Williams, *Sisters in the Wilderness: The Challenge of Womanist God-Talk* (Maryknoll, N.Y.: Orbis Books, 1993), 5–6.

43. A. Elaine Brown Crawford, *Hope in the Holler: A Womanist Theology* (Louisville: Westminster John Knox Press, 2002), xii.

44. Fett, *Working Cures*, 36.

45. Avery, *An Altar of Words*, 153.

Chapter 2 / Mamas and Aunties

1. Nina Bernstein, "Bronx Woman Convicted in Starving of Her Breast-Fed Son," *New York Times*, May 20, 1999, B-8.

2. Sondra O'Neale, "Inhibiting Midwives, Usurping Creators: The Struggling Emergence of Black Women in American Fiction," in *Feminist Studies, Critical Studies*, ed. Teresa de Lauretis (Bloomington: Indiana University Press), 141.

3. Walter Johnson, *Soul by Soul: Life inside the Antebellum Slave Market* (Cambridge: Harvard University Press, 1999), 19–24.

4. Angela Y. Davis, "Surrogates and Outcast Mothers: Racism and Reproductive Politics," in *It Just Ain't Fair: The Ethics of Health Care for African Americans*, ed. Annette Dula and Sara Goering (Westport, Conn.: Praeger, 1994), 44.

5. Diane Roberts, "The Value of Black Mothers' Work," *Radical America* 26, no. 1 (1996): 12.

6. Barbara Ehrenreich and Frances Fox Piven, "Without a Safety Net," *Mother Jones* 27, no. 3 (May–June 2002): 41.

7. Brett Williams, "Babies and Banks: The 'Reproductive Underclass' and the Raced, Gendered Masking of Debt," in *Race*, ed. Steven Gregory and Roger Sanjek (New Brunswick, N.J.: Rutgers University Press, 1994), 350.

8. Traci C. West, *Wounds of the Spirit: Black Women, Violence, and Resistance Ethics* (New York: New York University Press, 1999), 135.

9. National Vital Statistics Report, vol. 50, no. 5, February 12, 2002, 9.

10. Jason M. Fields and Lynn M. Casper, "America's Families and Living Arrangements," Current Population Reports, U.S. Census Bureau, Issued June 2001, 7.

11. Ibid., 7–8.

12. Carol Boyce Davies, "Mothering and Healing in Recent Black Women's Fiction," *Sage* 2, no. 1 (Spring 1985): 41.

13. Ibid., 43.

14. Sidney W. Mintz and Richard Price, *The Birth of African American Culture: An Anthropological Perspective* (Boston: Beacon Press, 1976, Preface, 1992), 10.

15. Sylvia Ardyn Boone, *Radiance from the Waters: Ideals of Feminine Beauty in Mende Art* (New Haven: Yale University Press, 1986), 82.

16. Ibid., 110.

17. Ibid., 141.

18. Patricia Hill Collins, *Black Feminist Thought: Knowledge, Consciousness, and the Politics of Empowerment* (New York: Routledge, 1990), 118.

19. Joyce West Stevens, *Smart and Sassy: The Strengths of Inner-City Black Girls* (New York: Oxford University Press, 2002), 66, 68.

20. Ibid., 74.

21. Ibid.

22. Joanne M. Braxton, "Black Grandmothers: Sources of Artistic Consciousness and Personal Strength," Working Paper 172, Wellesley College, Center for Research on Women, 1987, 3.

23. Traci C. West, *Wounds of the Spirit*, 167.

24. Patti LaBelle with Laura B. Randolph, *Don't Block the Blessings: Revelations of a Lifetime* (New York: Riverhead Books, 1996), 216.

25. Ibid., 281.

26. Mary C. Lewis, *Herstory: Black Female Rites of Passage* (Chicago: African American Images, 1988), 101–14.

27. Adrienne Johnson, "Going to Ghana," in *Go Girl! The Black Woman's Book of Adventure and Travel*, ed. Elaine Lee (Portland, Ore.: Eighth Mountain Press, 1997), 27.

28. Cheryl Townsend Gilkes, *"If It Wasn't for the Women . . .": Black Women's Experience and Womanist Culture in Church and Community* (Maryknoll, N.Y.: Orbis Books, 2001), 102–3.

29. Patricia Hill Collins, *Black Feminist Thought: Knowledge, Consciousness, and the Politics of Empowerment* (New York: Routledge, 1991), 119.

30. Karen Baker-Fletcher and Garth Baker-Fletcher, *My Sister, My Brother: Womanist and Xodus God-Talk* (Maryknoll, N.Y.: Orbis Books, 1997), 177.

31. Ibid., 177–78.

32. Toinette M. Eugene, "There Is a Balm in Gilead: Black Women and the Black Church as Agents of a Therapeutic Community," in *Women's Spirituality, Women's Lives in Women and Therapy*, vol. 16, no. 2/3, ed. Judith Ochshorn and Ellen Cole (New York: Haworth Press, 1995), 66.

33. Gilkes, *"If It Wasn't for the Women...,"* 103.

34. Darlene Clark Hine, *Hinesight: Black Women and the Re-Construction of American History* (Brooklyn: Carlson Publishing, 1994), xxii.

35. See, for example, Deborah Gray White, *Ar'n't I a Woman? Female Slaves in the Plantation South* (New York: W. W. Norton, 1985).

36. Lalita Tademy, *Cane River* (New York: Warner Books, 2002).

37. Ibid., xi.

38. Ibid., xv.

39. Yvette Abrahams, "Colonialism, Dysjuncture, and Dysfunction: Sara Bartmann's Resistance," unpublished paper presented at the AGI informal seminar series, November 6, 2001, 1.

40. Angela M. Gilliam, "Sexual Commodification of Women," in *Black Feminist Anthropology: Theory, Politics, Praxis, and Poetics*, ed. Irma McClaurin (New Brunswick, N.J.: Rutgers University Press, 2001).

41. Yvette Abrahams, "Ambiguity Is My Middle Name: A Research Diary," excerpt from *Colonialism, Dysfunction and Dysjuncture: The Historiography of Sarah Bartmann*, Ph.D. thesis, Department of History, University of Cape Town, 2000, 7.

42. Ibid., 12, 33.

Chapter 3 / Granny Midwives and Girlfriends

1. Marie Jenkins Schwartz, "'Oh How I Ran': Breast-feeding and Weaning on Plantation and Farm in Antebellum Virginia and Alabama," in *Discovering the Women in Slavery*, ed. Patricia Morton (Athens: University of Georgia Press, 1996), 246.

2. Martia Graham Goodson, "Medical-Botanical Contributions of African Slave Women to American Medicine," in *Black Women in American History*, ed. Darlene Clark Hine (New York: Carlson Publishing, 1990), 2.

3. Todd L. Savitt, *Medicine and Slavery: The Diseases and Health Care of Blacks in Antebellum Virginia* (Urbana: University of Illinois Press, 1978), 182.

4. Deborah Gray White, *Ar'n't I a Woman? Female Slaves in the Plantation South* (New York: W. W. Norton, 1985), 119.

5. Valerie Lee, *Granny Midwives and Black Women Writers: Double-Dutched Readings* (New York: Routledge, 1996), 5.

6. White, *Ar'n't I a Woman?* 98.

7. Lee, *Granny Midwives and Black Women Writers*, 90.

8. Sheila P. Davis and Cora A. Ingram, "Empowered Caretakers: A Historical Perspective on the Roles of Granny Midwives in Rural Alabama," in *Wings of Gauze: Women of Color and the Experience of Health and Illness*, ed. Barbara Bair and Susan E. Cayleff (Detroit: Wayne State University Press, 1993), 193.

9. Gloria Waite, "Childbirth, Lay Institution Building, and Health Polity: The Traditional Childbearing Group, Inc., of Boston in a Historical Context," in *Wings of Gauze: Women of Color and the Experience of Health and Illness*, ed. Barbara Bair and Susan E. Cayleff (Detroit: Wayne State University Press, 1993), 207.

10. Davis and Ingram, "Empowered Caretakers," 196.

11. Katherine Clark, "Introduction" to Onnie Lee Logan, *Motherwit: An Alabama Midwife's Story* (New York: Plume Books, 1991), xi.

12. Ibid.

13. Onnie Lee Logan as told to Katherine Clark, *Motherwit: An Alabama Midwife's Story* (New York: Plume Books, 1991), 90.

14. Ibid., 91.

15. Ibid., 102.

16. Ibid., 130–31.

17. Ibid., 89–90.

18. Margaret Charles Smith and Linda Janet Holmes, *Listen to Me Good: The Life Story of an Alabama Midwife* (Columbus: Ohio State University Press, 1996), 104.

19. Ibid., 52–53.

20. Ibid., 90–91.

21. Ibid., 34.

22. Linda Villarosa, ed., *Body and Soul: The Black Women's Guide to Physical Health and Emotional Well-Being* (New York: HarperCollins Publishers, 1994), 254.

23. Davis and Ingram, "Empowered Caretakers," 199.

24. bell hooks, "Save Your Breath, Sisters," *New York Times*, January 7, 1996.

25. Opal Palmer Adisa, "Rocking in the Sun Light: Stress and Black Women," in *The Black Women's Health Book: Speaking for Ourselves*, rev. ed., ed. Evelyn C. White (Seattle: Seal Press, 1994), 12.

26. Ibid.

27. Traci C. West, *Wounds of the Spirit: Black Women, Violence, and Resistance Ethics* (New York: New York University Press, 1999), 183.

28. Villarosa, *Body and Soul*, 385–86.

29. Charlotte Watson Sherman, "An Anointing: Sisterfriends," in *Sisterfire: Black Womanist Fiction and Poetry*, ed. Charlotte Watson Sherman (New York: Harper Perennial, 1994), 161.

Chapter 4 / Healing in Love

1. This view has been prevalent in spirituality studies developed by authors such as Daniel J. Levinson and Erik Erikson in their human developmental theories. For a refutation of these ideas from a feminist perspective, see Carol Gilligan, "In a Different Voice: Visions of Maturity," in *Women's Spirituality: Resources for Christian Development*, ed. Joann Wolski Conn (New York: Paulist Press, 1986), 63–87.

2. Jacquelyn Grant, "The Sin of Servanthood and the Deliverance of Discipleship," in *A Troubling in My Soul: Womanist Perspectives on Evil and Suffering,* ed. Emilie M. Townes (Maryknoll, N.Y.: Orbis Books, 1993), 199–218.

3. Kristin Koptiuch, "Third-Worlding at Home," in *Culture, Power, Place: Explorations in Critical Anthropology,* ed. Akhil Gupta and James Ferguson (Durham, N.C.: Duke University Press, 1999), 237.

4. Philip N. Cohen, "Racial-Ethnic and Gender Differences in Returns to Cohabitation and Marriage: Evidence from the Current Population Survey," Population Division, U.S. Bureau of the Census, Population Division Working Paper 35 (Washington, D.C., May 1999), 1.

5. Ibid., 7.

6. Ibid., 8; emphasis added.

7. "The Negro Family: The Case for National Action," Office of Policy Planning and Research, U.S. Department of Labor (Washington, D.C.: March 1965), 2.

8. Paul Finkleman, "Crimes of Love, Misdemeanors of Passion," in *The Devil's Lane: Sex and Race in the Early South,* ed. Catherine Clinton and Michele Gillespie (New York: Oxford University Press, 1997), 131.

9. Ann L. Stoler, "Making Empire Respectable: The Politics of Race and Sexual Morality in Twentieth-Century Colonial Cultures," in *Situated Lives: Gender and Culture in Everyday Life,* ed. Louise Lamphere, Helen Ragoné, and Patricia Zavella (New York: Routledge, 1997), 374.

10. Carolyn Martin Shaw, "Disciplining the Black Female Body: Learning Feminism in Africa and the United States" in *Black Feminist Anthropology: Theory, Politics, Praxis, and Poetics,* ed. Irma McClaurin (New Brunswick, N.J.: Rutgers University Press, 2001), 109.

11. bell hooks, *Killing Rage: Ending Racism* (New York: Henry Holt and Company, 1995), 71.

12. Traci C. West, *Wounds of the Spirit: Black Women, Violence and Resistance Ethics* (New York: New York University Press), 103–4.

13. Delores S. Williams, "The Color of Feminism: Or Speaking the Black Woman's Tongue," *Journal of Religious Thought* 43 (1986): 54.

14. Cheryl Rodriguez, "A Homegirl Goes Home," in *Black Feminist Anthropology: Theory, Politics, Praxis, and Poetics,* ed. Irma McClaurin (New Brunswick, N.J.: Rutgers University Press, 2001), 239.

15. Cheryl Townsend Gilkes, "Ministry to Women: Hearing and Empowering 'Poor' Black Women," in *One Third of a Nation: African American Perspectives,* ed. Ura Jean Oyemade Bailey and Lorenzo Morris (Washington, D.C.: Howard University Press, 2001), 201–2.

16. Cited in West, *Wounds of the Spirit,* 103.

17. Bakari Kitwana, *The Hip Hop Generation: Young Blacks and the Crisis in African-American Culture* (New York: BasicCivitas Books, 2002), 97–104.

18. Kelly Brown Douglas, *Sexuality and the Black Church: A Womanist Perspective* (Maryknoll, N.Y.: Orbis Books, 1999), 68.

19. Bishop T. D. Jakes, *The Lady, Her Lover, and Her Lord* (New York: G. P. Putnam Sons, 1998), 132.

20. Stephan Thernstrom and Abigail Thernstrom, "Black Family Structure and Poverty," in *Feuds about Families: Conservative, Centrist, Liberal, and Feminist Perspectives*, ed. Nijole V. Benokraitis (Englewood, N.J.: Prentice Hall, 2000), 264.

21. Ibid.

22. Kitwana, *The Hip Hop Generation*, 116.

23. Benoit Denizet-Lewis, "Double Lives on the Down Low," *New York Times Magazine*, August 3, 2003, 30.

24. Douglas, *Sexuality and the Black Church*, 105.

25. Jacquie Bishop, "In Memory of Sakia Gunn," www.keithboykin.com/arch/000741.html, May 16, 2003.

26. Kelly Cogswell and Ana Simo, "Erasing Sakia: Who's to Blame?" *The Gully*, www.thegully.com, June 6, 2003.

27. Renita J. Weems, *I Asked for Intimacy: Stories of Blessings, Betrayals, and Birthings* (San Diego: LuraMedia, 1993), 100.

Chapter 5 / Sexuality, Hazard, and Hope

1. Michael Moore, *Stupid White Men* (New York: Harper Collins, 2001), 59, 60.

2. Jacqueline Battalora, "The Workings of an Ideology," in *Gender, Ethnicity, and Religion: Views from the Other Side*, ed. Rosemary Radford Ruether (Minneapolis: Fortress Press, 2002), 16.

3. Cheryl A. Kirk-Duggan, "Humpty Dumpty Need Not Fall Again: A Theo-Poetics of Holistic Health," *Journal of Women and Religion* 20 (2002): 128–29.

4. Angela Y. Davis, *Violence against Women and the Ongoing Challenge to Racism* (Latham, N.Y.: Kitchen Table, Women of Color Press, 1985), 11.

5. Linda Villarosa, ed., *Body and Soul: The Black Woman's Guide to Physical Health and Emotional Well-Being* (New York: Harper Perennial, 1994), 524.

6. Marc H. Morial, Keynote Address, National Urban League convention, Pittsburgh, July 27, 2003.

7. Beth Richie, *Compelled to Crime: The Gender Entrapment of Battered Black Women* (New York: Routledge, 1996), 141.

8. Ibid., 145.

9. Ibid., 163.

10. Villarosa, *Body and Soul*, 499–500.

11. Tricia Rose, *Longing to Tell: Black Women Talk about Sexuality and Intimacy* (New York: Farrar, Straus, and Giroux, 2003), 390.

12. Alice Walker, "Coming Apart," in *Take Back the Night*, ed. L. Lederer (New York: William Morrow, 1980), 103. Cited in Alice Mayall and Diana E. Russell, "Racism in Pornography," *Feminism and Psychology* 3, no. 2 (June 1993): 277.

13. Mayall and Russell, "Racism in Pornography," 280.

14. Bakari Kitwana, *The Hip Hop Generation: Young Blacks and the Crisis in African-American Culture* (New York: BasicCivitas Books, 2002), 113, 114.

15. Villarosa, *Body and Soul*, 501, 503.

16. Kitwana, *The Hip Hop Generation*, 99–101.

17. Gail Elizabeth Wyatt, *Stolen Women: Reclaiming Our Sexuality, Taking Back Our Lives* (New York: John Wiley and Sons, 1999), 143.

18. Melba Wilson, *Crossing the Boundary: Black Women Survive Incest* (Seattle: Seal Press, 1994), 7.

19. Ibid., 13, 14.

20. Wyatt, *Stolen Women*, 43.

21. Benoit Denizet-Lewis, "Double Lives on the Down Low," *New York Times Magazine*, August 3, 2003, 30.

22. Statistics courtesy of Sexuality Information and Education Council of the United States (SIECUS), presentation at Auburn Theological Seminary, New York City, July 27, 2003. For more information, www.siecus.org.

23. Beth Richie, "AIDS: In Living Color," in *The Black Women's Health Book: Speaking for Ourselves*, ed. Evelyn C. White (Seattle: Seal, 1994), 184.

24. Denizet-Lewis, "Double Lives on the Down Low," 52.

25. Richie, "AIDS: In Living Color," 183–84.

26. Mari J. Matsuda, *Where Is Your Body? And Other Essays on Race, Gender, and the Law* (Boston: Beacon Press, 1996), 124.

27. Rose, *Longing to Tell*, 400.

28. Information courtesy of Sexuality Information and Education Council of the United States (SIECUS).

29. Wyatt, *Stolen Women*, 81.

30. Farah Jasmine Griffin, "Conflict and Chaos," in *Is It Nation Time? Contemporary Essays on Black Power and Black Nationalism*, ed. Eddie S. Glaude Jr. (Chicago: University of Chicago Press, 2002), 120.

31. Rose, *Longing to Tell*, 390.

Chapter 6 / African American Women and White Health Institutions

1. Tera Hunter, *To 'Joy My Freedom: Southern Black Women's Lives and Labors after the Civil War* (Cambridge, Mass.: Harvard University Press, 1997), 204.

2. Ibid., 187.

3. Ibid., 205.

4. Ibid., 189.

5. Susan Smith, *Sick and Tired of Being Sick and Tired: Black Women's Health Activism in America, 1890–1950* (Philadelphia: University of Pennsylvania Press, 1995), 47.

6. Cited in ibid., 42.

7. Ibid., 41.

8. Ibid., 66–70.

9. *National Negro Health News*, United States Public Health Service, 1, no. 1 (January–March 1933): 1.

10. Ibid.

11. Smith, *Sick and Tired of Being Sick and Tired,* 118.

12. *National Negro Health News,* Federal Security Agency, Public Health Service, 18, no. 2 (April–June 1950): 1.

13. Evelyn Brooks Higginbotham, *Righteous Discontent: The Women's Movement in the Black Baptist Church, 1880–1920* (Cambridge, Mass.: Harvard University Press, 1993), 196.

14. Ibid., 195.

15. Ibid., 207–29.

16. Paula Giddings, *When and Where I Enter: The Impact of Black Women on Race and Sex in America* (New York: Bantam Books, 1985), 19.

17. *Proceedings of the National Negro Conference 1909* (New York: Arno Press and the *New York Times,* 1969), 175.

18. Floris Barnett Cash, *African American Women and Social Action: The Clubwomen and Volunteerism from Jim Crow to the New Deal, 1896–1936* (Westport, Conn.: Greenwood Press, 2001), 12.

19. Giddings, *When and Where I Enter,* 104, 105.

20. Smith, *Sick and Tired of Being Sick and Tired,* 20–25.

21. Francis H. Warren, comp., *Michigan Manual of Freedmen's Progress* (1915 reprint; Detroit: John M. Green, 1985), 141–42.

22. Pamela Martin, Sinead Younge, and Aisha Smith, "Searching for a Balm in Gilead: The HIV/AIDS Epidemic and the African American Church," *African American Research Perspectives* (Winter 2003): 70; emphasis added.

23. Sheila Battle, "Moving Targets: Alcohol, Crack and Black Women," in *The Black Women's Health Book: Speaking for Ourselves,* ed. Evelyn C. White (Seattle: Seal, 1994), 255.

24. Carl V. Hill, Rashid S. Njai, Harold W. Neighbors, David R. Williams, and James S. Jackson, "Racial Discrimination and the Physical Health of Black Americans: Review of the Literature on Community Studies of Race and Health," *African American Research Perspectives* 9, no. 1 (Winter 2003): 12.

25. Alvin F. Poussaint and Amy Alexander, *Lay My Burden Down: Unraveling Suicide and the Mental Health Crisis among African-Americans* (Boston: Beacon Press, 2000), 18.

26. Ibid., 15.

27. Anonymous, "The Strong Black Woman Is Dead."

28. Dorothy Roberts, *Killing the Black Body: Race, Reproduction, and the Meaning of Liberty* (New York: Vintage Books, 1999), 234.

29. Karen DeWitt, "Turning Chaos into Calm," *Essence* 33, no. 9 (January 2003): 99–102.

30. Jeannine Amber, "Why Don't You Use a Condom?" *Essence* 33, no. 4 (August 2002): 118–22.

31. Kristal Brent Zook, "Saving a Southern Town in the Grip of AIDS," *Essence* 33, no. 10 (February 2003): 130–37.

32. Jan Willis, "One Love, One Faith, Two Baptisms," *Heart and Soul* 9, no. 8 (October 2002): 48–49.

33. Ayana Byrd, "Let's Make a Deal," *Heart and Soul* 9, no. 8 (October 2002): 68–70.

34. Ayana Byrd, "Spirit Warriors," *Heart and Soul* 9, no. 8 (October 2002): 32–36.

35. Queen Afua, *Sacred Woman: A Guide to Healing the Feminine Body, Mind, and Spirit* (New York: One World, 2000), 11–12.

36. Ibid., 32.

Chapter 7 / Womanist Explorations

1. Toinette M. Eugene, "In This Here Place, We Flesh: Womanist Ruminations on Embodied Experience and Expressions," *Daughters of Sarah* 22, no. 1 (Winter 1996): 14–15.

2. Alita Anderson, *On the Other Side: African Americans Tell of Healing* (Louisville: Westminster John Knox Press, 2001).

3. Delores Williams, *Sisters in the Wilderness: The Challenge of Womanist God-Talk* (Maryknoll, N.Y.: Orbis Books, 1993), 2–8, 14–33.

4. Renita J. Weems, *Just a Sister Away: A Womanist Vision of Women's Relationships in the Bible* (San Diego: LuraMedia, 1988), 2.

5. Patricia J. Williams, *The Alchemy of Race and Rights: Diary of a Law Professor* (Cambridge, Mass.: Harvard University Press, 1991), 73.

6. Toinette Eugene, "While Love Is Unfashionable: Ethical Implications of Black Spirituality and Sexuality," in *Sexuality and the Sacred: Sources for Theological Reflection*, ed. James B. Nelson and Sandra P. Longfellow (Louisville: Westminster John Knox Press, 1994), 107.

7. Ibid., 108.

8. A. Elaine Brown Crawford, *Hope in the Holler: A Womanist Theology* (Louisville: Westminster John Knox Press, 2002), 117.

9. Byllye Avery, *An Altar of Words: Wisdom, Comfort, and Inspiration for African American Women* (New York: Broadway Books, 1998), 73.

10. Alvin F. Poussaint and Amy Alexander, *Lay My Burden Down: Unraveling Suicide and the Mental Health Crisis among African-Americans* (Boston: Beacon Press, 2000), 131–32.

11. Cheryl Townsend Gilkes, *"If It Wasn't for the Women...": Black Women's Experience and Womanist Culture in Church and Community* (Maryknoll, N.Y.: Orbis Books, 2001), 4.

12. Ibid., 25–26.

INDEX